Argentina

Argentina

BY JEAN F. BLASHFIELD

Enchantment of the World
Second Series

Children's Press®

A Division of Scholastic Inc.

NEW YORK TORONTO LONDON AUCKLAND SYDNEY
MEXICO CITY NEW DELHI HONG KONG
DANBURY, CONNECTICUT

Frontispiece: Los Glaciares National Park, Patagonia

Consultant: Ricky Abisla, Civic Council of Grassroots and Indigenous
Groups of Honduras

Please note: All statistics are as up-to-date as possible at the time of publication.

Book production by Herman Adler

Library of Congress Cataloging-in-Publication Data

Blashfield, Jean F.
  Argentina / by Jean F. Blashfield.
    p. cm. — (Enchantment of the world. Second series)
  ISBN-13: 978-0-516-24872-1
  ISBN-10: 0-516-24872-3
  1. Argentina—Juvenile literature. I. Title. II. Series.
  F2808.2.B56 2007
  982—dc22   2006006037

Argentina

Contents

Cover photo:
Iguassu Falls

Herding sheep

The tango

"Where the Land Ends and the Sky Begins"

"THE PLAINS, THE WOODS, THE RIVERS, ARE ALL IMMENSE; and the horizon is always undefined, always lost in haze . . . that forbid the eye to mark the point in the distance . . . , where the land ends and the sky begins." That's how Domingo F. Sarmiento, one of Argentina's founding fathers, once described his country.

Sarmiento was writing sometime about 1845, when Argentina had become an independent nation but had not yet become the envy of other nations. Soon, Argentines would take advantage of their greatest resource, a huge grassland

Opposite: **In western Argentina, the Andes Mountains tower over vast flatlands.**

A horse skull sits among the grasses of the Pampas. *Pampa* **means "level plain" in the Quechua language.**

called the Pampas. In the coming decades, its farm products would be shipped all over the globe, and Argentina would become one of the world's wealthiest nations. The Argentines built Buenos Aires, one of the world's great cities, on the Atlantic coast, between the sea and the Pampas.

Argentina stretches out across South America. It shares the southern half of the continent with the long, skinny country of Chile. South America gets narrower and narrower toward its southern end. This region is sometimes called the Southern Cone because it is shaped like an ice cream cone. The "ice cream" top of the Southern Cone is the Pampas. Part of the "cone" is a region called Patagonia. Patagonia was long

Parts of Patagonia are desolate wilderness. The dry land supports few trees.

The towering Andes Mountains mark Argentina's western border. Thirty peaks in Argentina rise to more than 20,000 feet (6,100 m).

considered an unknown and unknowable wilderness. Both the Pampas and Patagonia are generally flat, but they gradually rise to the foothills of the great Andes Mountains. This huge, high mountain chain runs along the border between Argentina and Chile.

A book published in 1612 called part of southern South America *Tierra Argentina*, meaning "Land of Silver." This name arose because of legends about the land around Río de La

Some Words About Argentina

The people of Argentina are called Argentines. Argentina is a Latin American country, as are all countries in the Western Hemisphere south of the United States. It is also a South American country. South America includes everything south of Panama. Most of South America, including Argentina, is in the Southern Hemisphere, south of the equator.

People from Latin American countries are often called Hispanics, meaning that they speak Spanish and are of Spanish heritage. Most Argentines, however, trace their roots back to Italy, France, Greece, or another country, rather than Spain. Argentines do speak Spanish, which is the nation's official language.

The inhabitants of Buenos Aires and the area around it are called *porteños*, meaning "people of the port." Everything beyond Buenos Aires is called the Interior, and its inhabitants are usually called *campesinos*, which means "farmers."

Buenos Aires boasts the largest port in South America.

Plata, the great bay on which Buenos Aires is located. The legends held that a great mountain of silver could be found in this region. The Spaniards who explored the area never found a mountain of silver. But they did find much fertile land.

A hundred years ago, many people thought that Argentina would become just like the United States. It was viewed as a modern land filled with promise and economic opportunity. Millions of Europeans moved to Argentina to enjoy that opportunity. But Argentina has not turned into a second United States. Instead, it has remained its own country. It accepts influences from all over the world, and it turns them into something uniquely Argentine.

At the beginning of the twenty-first century, Argentina is no longer thought of as a southern version of the United States. Instead, it is a great Latin American country.

That Little Accent Mark

Some words in Spanish have an accent mark. When you see an accent mark, you give the syllable it is on more emphasis than you give the other syllables. In some small words the accent mark gives the word a different meaning. For example, *si* means "yes," but *si* means "if."

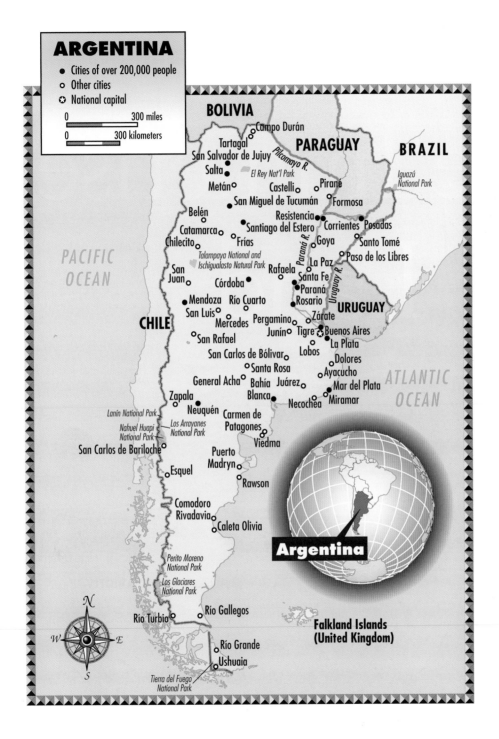

ARGENTINA

- ● Cities of over 200,000 people
- ○ Other cities
- ✪ National capital

0   300 miles
0   300 kilometers

BOLIVIA

Campo Durán

Tartagal

PARAGUAY

San Salvador de Jujuy

Pilcomayo R.

BRAZIL

Salta

El Rey Nat'l Park

Metán

Castelli

Piraná

Iguazú National Park

San Miguel de Tucumán

Formosa

Belén

Resistencia

Corrientes

Posadas

Catamarca

Santiago del Estero

Chilecito

Frías

Paraná R.

Goya

Santo Tomé

Talampaya National and Ischigualasto Natural Park

Rafaela

La Paz

Paso de los Libres

San Juan

Córdoba

Santa Fe

Paraná

Uruguay R.

PACIFIC OCEAN

Mendoza

Río Cuarto

Rosario

URUGUAY

San Luis

Zárate

Mercedes

Pergamino

Tigre

Buenos Aires

CHILE

Junín

La Plata

San Rafael

Lobos

San Carlos de Bólivar

Dolores

Santa Rosa

Ayacucho

General Acha

Bahía

Juárez

Mar del Plata

Blanca

Miramar

ATLANTIC OCEAN

Zapala

Necochea

Neuquén

Carmen de Patagones

Lanín National Park

Viedma

Nahuel Huapi National Park

Los Arrayanes National Park

San Carlos de Bariloche

Puerto Madryn

Esquel

Rawson

Comodoro Rivadavia

Caleta Olivia

Argentina

Perito Moreno National Park

Los Glaciares National Park

Río Gallegos

Río Turbio

Falkland Islands (United Kingdom)

N

W   E

S

Río Grande

Ushuaia

Tierra del Fuego National Park

The Immense Land

A RGENTINA IS IMMENSE. WITH A TOTAL AREA OF 1,068,020 square miles (2,765,958 square kilometers), it is the eighth-largest nation in the world and the second-largest in South America, trailing only Brazil. Argentina's vast space is filled with majestic scenery—ice-covered mountains, seemingly endless plains, frozen, treeless tundra, and dramatic rain forests.

Argentina is bordered by five countries and the Atlantic Ocean. The border in the northwest is with Bolivia. Paraguay and Brazil are to the northeast. Uruguay is tucked in between Argentina, Brazil, and the Atlantic Ocean. Chile borders Argentina to the west and then wraps around the southern "toe" of the country. Argentina also has a long coastline, stretching 3,098 miles (4,986 km) from Buenos Aires south to the cold islands of Tierra del Fuego.

Opposite: **A series of lakes grace Nahuel Huapi National Park in Patagonia.**

Valdés Peninsula is famed for its cliffs that rise straight from the sea.

Argentina's Lake District lies along the border with Chile. Its striking deep blue lakes make it a year-round vacation spot for Argentines.

This big country has many different kinds of landscape. The Interior is made up of five regions—the Andes, the North, Mesopotamia, the Pampas, and Patagonia. In addition, there are the coast and Buenos Aires itself.

The Río de la Plata as seen from space. The huge estuary is 136 miles (220 km) across at its widest point.

The Coast

Argentina's most significant river, the Río de la Plata ("River of Silver") is not actually a river. It is the estuary formed where the Paraná and Uruguay rivers join and flow into the Atlantic Ocean. An estuary is a bay where the salt water from the ocean mingles with the freshwater carried by rivers. The natural estuary of Río de la Plata was not very deep, but in the nineteenth century, laborers dug out the bottom and removed many shallow islands so that ships could travel safely. Today, Buenos Aires, which is located on the bay, is the largest port in South America.

Argentina's Geographic Features

Highest Point: Mount Aconcagua, 22,835 feet (6,960 m)

Lowest Point: Laguna del Carbón, 345 feet (105 m) below sea level

Largest City (2005 estimate): Buenos Aires, 11,600,000

Longest River: Paraná, the second-longest river system in South America, though only part of it is in Argentina

Longest Border: With Chile, 3,200 miles (5,150 km)

Largest Lake: Lake Argentino, 570 square miles (1,470 sq km)

Highest Average Temperature: 90°F (32°C) in January in Mendoza region

Lowest Average Temperature: 27°F (3°C) in July in southern Patagonia

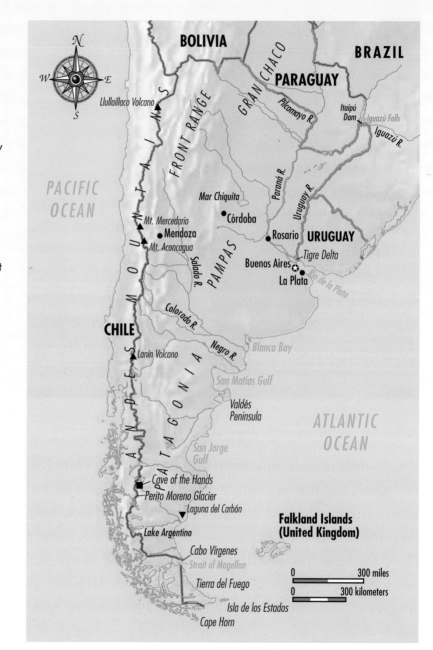

The Andes

The Andes Mountains form a great wall along Argentina's western border with Chile. These towering mountains rise to an average height of 13,000 feet (4,000 meters). They run north to south all the way to Tierra del Fuego, islands off South America's tip that are split between Chile and Argentina. The farther south the mountains are, the more likely they are to have permanent glaciers, or ice sheets, on their tops.

Jagged peaks pierce the clouds in the southern Andes. The Andes are the world's second-highest mountain range, trailing only the Himalaya in Asia.

The Andes Mountains were formed by the movement of tectonic plates, giant pieces of Earth's crust. Tectonic plates are constantly moving. As they grind together, land is forced upward and volcanoes form. At least thirteen volcanoes in the Andes are still active. Several of them are shared with Chile, including Llullaillaco, which last erupted in 1877. It rises to a height of 22,057 feet (6,723 m), making it the second-highest volcano in the world.

Regions where two tectonic plates meet are more likely to suffer earthquakes. Many earthquakes have been felt in Tucumán and Mendoza provinces in northwestern Argentina. Sometimes this violent jarring of the earth can be felt more than 500 miles (800 km) away in Buenos Aires.

The Highest Peak

The highest point in Argentina is Mount Aconcagua, which means "Sentinel of Stone." Soaring to 22,835 feet (6,960 m), it is the highest peak in both the Western Hemisphere and the Southern Hemisphere. In 1897, a Swiss man named Mathias Zurbriggen became the first European to climb Mount Aconcagua. But there is evidence that indigenous, or native, people from South America had climbed it much earlier. Mount Aconcagua is located a little to the east of the Andes Mountains, in what is called the Front Range. The mountain has two peaks, one 95 feet (29 m) higher than the other.

The Statue in the Mountains

In 1902, Argentina and Chile came close to going to war over their border. People in both countries urged their governments to find a peaceful way to solve the conflict. The two countries agreed and let the U.S. ambassador and the British king decide on the border. Argentines and Chileans accepted their decision peaceably. To commemorate this, in 1904 a huge statue of Jesus called *Christ of the Andes* was erected at 13,000 feet (4,000 m) on the border between the two nations.

The North and Mesopotamia

In northern Argentina, a dry land called the Gran Chaco spills over into Bolivia and Paraguay. Few people live on this hot, arid plain. Scrubby forests cover parts of the Gran Chaco. The quebracho tree abounds in these forests. It has unusually hard wood. (*Quebracho* means "ax breaker" in Spanish.) The tough wood is used to make telephone poles. The trees are also a source of tannin, a chemical used in tanning leather. It is extracted from the old wood in the center of the tree. Cutting quebracho trees is one of the Gran Chaco's most important industries, so the trees are becoming increasingly scarce. The Gran Chaco also produces cotton. Many workers from Bolivia and Paraguay cross the border to pick it.

Palms and other trees rise above the grasslands of the Gran Chaco. The hot, sometimes humid region is home to few people but many insects.

A salt lake called Mar Chiquita sits at the southern edge of the Gran Chaco. It is about 45 miles (70 km) long and so wide in places that you can't see across it. Salt marshes lie to the north.

To the east of the Gran Chaco is the region called Mesopotamia, which means "between the rivers." The two rivers are the Paraná and the Uruguay. Part of Mesopotamia juts northeastward between Brazil and Paraguay. Many tourists come to this hot and humid region because it is home to the world-famous Iguazú Falls, on the border between Argentina and Brazil.

The Pampas

The Pampas, or *Pampa* in Spanish, is one of the world's great grasslands. The name comes from a Quechua word meaning "level plain." The Pampas is quite flat except for a range of

"Great Water"

The Iguazú River flows from Brazil toward the Paraná River. Along the Argentine-Brazilian border, it breaks into 275 separate waterfalls that tumble over the edge of a plateau. Iguazú Falls is one of the world's most spectacular sites. The name *Iguazú* means "Great Water" in Guaraní, an indigenous language, and the roar from the crashing water is deafening. In total, the falls are about 2 miles (3 km) wide. Roughly 70 percent of the mighty falls are in Argentina and 30 percent are in Brazil. Iguazú Falls is located in a lush rain forest, and both countries have declared their section to be a national park.

hills in the south, which rises to about 4,000 feet (1,200 m). It covers about 230,000 square miles (600,000 sq km), nearly the size of Texas.

The Pampas can be divided into two parts by climate—the dry land and the wet land. The eastern portion is wetter and thus grows taller grasses and some trees. This part of the Pampas gets enough rain to support the country's main crops of wheat, corn, sorghum, soybeans, and sugar beets. Lower grasses and fewer trees grow in the much drier western portion. Beef cattle and horses by the millions roam these open plains. Cowboys called gauchos keep an eye on the cattle.

A Look at Argentina's Cities

Buenos Aires is Argentina's largest city and capital. Córdoba (below), Argentina's second-largest city, is the nation's educational center. It has seven universities, including Argentina's oldest, the University of Córdoba. Founded in 1573, Córdoba still has much of the architecture from its early years. But it is also a modern, rapidly growing city. Manufacturing is important, especially of cars, airplanes, and agricultural machinery.

Rosario, located northwest of Buenos Aires on the banks of the Paraná River, is the nation's third-largest city. It has a long, welcoming, beach-filled waterfront called La Costanera. Both a port and a railway center, Rosario is an important hub for shipping agricultural products.

Mendoza, the fourth-largest city, is the center of Argentina's wine-growing region. Located on a main road to Chile, it is the setting-off point for visits to Mount Aconcagua. The Mendoza River is swift and popular with white-water rafters. Although the city is often hot and humid, a wealth of trees keeps people comfortable.

La Plata (above), Argentina's fifth-largest city, is located in the northern Pampas on the banks of the Río de la Plata. The city's cathedral is the largest in Argentina. The National University of La Plata is widely known for its teaching of the sciences. The city's industries include meatpacking.

Patagonia

The far south of Argentina is a cooler area called Patagonia. In parts of Patagonia, permanent ice covers the land. In some places, huge ice sheets called glaciers move toward the sea. Chunks of the glaciers break off and fall into the ocean, becoming icebergs.

Patagonia extends eastward from the Andes Mountains and south from the Colorado River. It was named in 1520 when explorer Ferdinand Magellan saw Tehuelche people wearing extra-large boots. He called them *patagones*, meaning "big feet." The land descends from the Andes in a series of plateaus. Most of Patagonia is steppe—cold, dry grassland that cannot support trees. The soil is not fertile, so few people live there, but sheep abound. Deep, grassy valleys break up the plateaus of Patagonia. Some of these valleys produce fruit.

Most of Patagonia is too cold and dry to grow crops, but sheep can survive on the meager grasses. An estimated eight million sheep live in the region.

The Valdés Peninsula stretches out into the Atlantic Ocean in the northern part of Patagonia. It is famed for its incredible beauty and its wildlife, such as elephant seals and right whales. For many years, the lowest place in Argentina was thought to be Salinas Chicas ("Small Salt Mines") on the Valdés Peninsula. Salinas Chicas reaches 131 feet (40 m) below sea level. But parts of Patagonia are still being explored, and an even deeper spot, the lowest in all of South America, has been discovered.

Laguna del Carbón ("Carbon Lake") is located near the port of Santa Cruz in a canyon 345 feet (105 m) below sea level. That is lower than California's Death Valley.

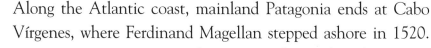

The Tip of the Continent

Ushuaia has sometimes been called the end of the world. Today, it is a top tourist spot.

Along the Atlantic coast, mainland Patagonia ends at Cabo Vírgenes, where Ferdinand Magellan stepped ashore in 1520.

The water to the south is the eastern end of the Strait of Magellan, which separates the mainland from a group of islands called Tierra del Fuego, or "Land of Fire." Magellan gave the area its name because he spotted fires burning on the islands.

Tierra del Fuego is a chain of islands. Only the eastern third of the chain belongs to Argentina. The rest belongs to Chile, which wraps around the bottom of Patagonia. Ushuaia, the capital of Argentina's province of Tierra del Fuego, is called the world's southernmost city. Ushuaia grew around a prison where people convicted of serious crimes were sent so they would be far away from everyone else. Today, the city is home to about fifty thousand people.

Argentines believe that the province of Tierra del Fuego includes parts of Antarctica and islands in the South Atlantic. But some other countries, including the United States, do not recognize Argentina's claims in Antarctica, which partially overlap those of the United Kingdom and Chile.

Argentina's National Parks

Argentina has twenty-eight national parks. Some of them were created to preserve certain kinds of scenery, others to preserve certain plants and animals.

Created in 1934, Nahuel Huapi National Park (below) was the first national park in South America.

The park, which lies in the foothills of the Andes, contains many large lakes. The park gets its name from the largest of these lakes, which covers 250 square miles (650 sq km) and is 1,500 feet (460 m) deep. The name means "Tiger Island" in the language of the indigenous Mapuche people.

Nahuel Huapi is one of a chain of national parks that runs along the Andes Mountains from Aconcagua in the north to Los Glaciares (Glacier National Park) in the south. Lanín National Park surrounds the Lanín volcano, which is famed for its perfect cone shape. Numerous lakes in the park are fed by the snows from the mountains.

At the far southern tip of Argentina is Tierra del Fuego National Park. Featuring barren, wind-swept islands, it is Argentina's only coastal national park.

The original name of Buenos Aires was Nuestra Señora Santa Maria del Buen Aire, meaning "Our Lady Saint Mary of the Fair Winds." Spanish explorer Juan Díaz de Solís gave it that name in 1580. He was honoring the winds that drove his ships up the Río de la Plata to safe harbor.

Not all of Argentina's winds are so pleasant. In Patagonia, strong, cold winds called *pamperos* roll down the Andes Mountains and head east during the winter months. Although

Seals and cormorants rest on the rocks in Tierra del Fuego.

Patagonia is not really near the Antarctic (Tierra del Fuego is about 2,000 miles [3,200 km] from Antarctica), chill winds during winter can carry the cold from the polar region to Argentina.

Seasons in the Southern Hemisphere are the opposite of those in the Northern Hemisphere. Winter in Argentina is from June through September, and summer is December through March. This means that Argentines go skiing in August and open Christmas presents in the summer.

Unlike Canada and North America, most parts of Argentina do not get big extremes in weather. The far north, especially in Misiones province, has warm summers and rain throughout the year. This region gets about 80 inches (200 centimeters) of rain each year. Since Patagonia is so far south, it seems as if it should be very cold, but in fact the relatively warm ocean water surrounding it moderates the climate.

The eastern Pampas gets about 40 inches (100 cm) of rain per year. The western part of the plains gets less than one-fourth that amount and suffers frequent droughts, long periods without rain.

The weather in Buenos Aires is mild year-round. Its average winter temperature is 51 degrees Fahrenheit (11 degrees Celsius), and its average summer temperature is 75°F (24°C). It does not get snow. But the Andes and the far south get plenty of snow. Ushuaia, in Tierra del Fuego, has an average of seven days of snow in July. Its average low winter temperature is −29°F (−34°C) in July, and its average high summer temperature is 58°F (14.5°C) in January.

Amazing Life

ARGENTINA IS A LARGE COUNTRY, STRETCHING MORE than 2,000 miles (3,200 km) from north to south. It has soaring peaks and broad plains. This incredible variety of land means that it has an incredible variety of plants and animals. The widest variety of wildlife is found in the north.

Opposite: **Jaguars are the largest cats in the Western Hemisphere. A small number survive in remote regions of Argentina.**

Wild Cats

One of Argentina's most famous animals is the jaguar. Jaguars are a little larger than African leopards and smaller than Asian tigers. A jaguar's coat has black circles around yellowish spots, though some jaguars are almost all black. A century

Pumas are silent and stealthy hunters. They leap on to the back of their prey, often breaking its neck with a single bite.

ago, these spectacular cats roamed from the southern United States through Patagonia, but today they are nearly extinct. They have been widely hunted for their fur and to protect cattle, which they sometimes kill.

Several other wild cats live in Argentina. The puma (which is also called the cougar or mountain lion) is a large

animal that comes out at night to hunt. It has powerful legs and can leap up to 40 feet (12 m). Both the Geoffrey's cat and the Pampas cat are spotted, but they are much smaller than the jaguar. They weigh only about 10 pounds (4.5 kilograms) whereas the jaguar weighs between 75 and 220 pounds (35 and 100 kg). These two cats occupy the same area, but the Geoffrey's cat hides under thick ground cover, while the Pampas cat roams more open grasslands.

Monkeys

South America's monkeys differ from those of Africa and Asia. One main difference is that they can hang upside down in trees by holding on with their tails. Most South American monkeys are found in the rain forests. Howler monkeys, which

Threatened Wildlife

At least thirty-five species of mammals in Argentina are threatened or endangered. The short-tailed chinchilla (right) is the most endangered mammal in the country. In fact, it may already be extinct in the wild. Chinchillas are small rodents, slightly larger than guinea pigs. They are famed for their extremely soft hair. Millions were killed in the nineteenth and early twentieth centuries to make fur coats. Other endangered mammals in Argentina include several species of whales, the Chacoan peccary, giant and pink fairy armadillos, giant and marine otters, and the South Andean huemul.

live in the treetops of northern Argentina's dense forests, are the loudest animals in the Western Hemisphere. The males' bellowing bark comes from their supersized vocal cords. They use the sound to locate and keep other males away.

Capuchin monkeys live in the mountain forests of northwestern Argentina. They are great leapers, traveling more than 15 feet (4.5 m) through the treetops in one bound. They use their grasping tails to help them leap.

Marmosets are small, heavily furred monkeys with long tails. Though originally from Brazil, the common marmoset can now be found living in Buenos Aires.

Howler monkeys live high in the trees of Argentina's rain forest. They feed on fruit, flowers, and leaves.

The Giant Anteater

The long, narrow head of the giant anteater houses a very long, sticky tongue that can reach into termite nests to gobble up the insects. The anteater's tongue can grow up to 2 feet (60 cm) long! The creature has strong claws that are used to tear apart the rock-hard termite nests. Standing on its hind legs, the anteater uses its claws to fight its enemies, the jaguar and puma. Three other species of anteaters live in northwestern Argentina, but they are much smaller.

Rodents

Two-thirds of all types of mammals in Argentina are rodents, creatures with front teeth that are well suited to gnawing on hard objects like nuts or wood. One of the most curious is the vizcacha, which looks like it is part rabbit and part squirrel. Vizcachas live in the drier part of the Pampas, where they dig burrows in the ground. These burrows can break the leg of running cattle and sheep. Vizcachas have soft fur and long tails. Their fur is valuable, though not as much as the fur of the smaller chinchilla, which lives farther west in the Andes. The chinchilla's fur is one of the softest furs known.

Vizcachas live in groups of up to fifty animals. Their large burrows have many different rooms and entrances.

The capybara is the world's largest rodent—some are as big as a sheep. Capybaras live in marshlands and swamps along the edges of rivers. Because capybaras provide good meat and excellent leather, they may someday be raised like cattle. The mara, or Patagonian cavy, looks like a rabbit, but it isn't. Instead, it's related to the guinea pig. The Patagonian hare is not really a hare, but another type of cavy called an agouti.

Capybaras have partially webbed feet and are strong swimmers. They can stay underwater for several minutes.

Is It a Rodent or Not?

The pudu looks like a rodent, but it is actually the smallest member of the deer family. It generally stands no more than 15 inches (38 cm) high at the shoulder. Because of its small size, the pudu can easily hide in dense rain forests. Pudus live in the much-visited Nahuel Huapi National Park, but since they usually come out only at night, few people see them.

Other Mammals

The huemul, or South Andean deer, lives high in the Andes. As forests have been cut down and roads built, the huemul's habitat has been broken up into smaller and smaller pieces. The deer is now severely endangered.

Peccaries are the only pigs native to the Americas. Three species live in northern Argentina: the collared peccary; the larger white-lipped peccary; and the Chacoan peccary, which was discovered by scientists in the 1970s. The white-lipped peccary is often found in herds.

The piglike tapir, which lives in wet lowlands, is actually more closely related to the rhinoceros and horse than to the pig. It has a long, flexible nose like an elephant's trunk. Because tapirs are good to eat, they are threatened in Argentina.

Chacoan peccaies live in hot, dry regions. Cactus is their main food.

Animals from Afar

Animals brought to Argentina from distant lands have sometimes caused ecological problems. European rabbits and hares were introduced to Argentina in the nineteenth century. They have now spread to many regions. The beaver is creating havoc in Tierra del Fuego. The beaver was introduced from Canada in the 1940s to create a new beaver fur industry. That industry failed, and now these rodents, which cut down trees and dam streams to build their homes, are gradually destroying the countryside.

The coati is a raccoon relative whose range runs all the way from the southern United States to Argentina. It has a long, striped tail and a pointed nose. Amazingly, its ankles can turn backward so that the creature can climb down while keeping its head up.

Armadillos are common in northern Argentina, especially in the Chaco. The tiny pink fairy armadillo, also called the lesser pichi ciego, is almost extinct. The giant armadillo, which can reach 5 feet (1.5 m) in length, is also endangered. The most common armadillo is the same one found in Texas, the nine-banded armadillo.

Argentine Dinosaurs

The dry plains of Patagonia are a treasure trove for dinosaur hunters. Perhaps the largest dinosaur that ever lived was *Argentinosaurus*. It weighed as much as 100 tons and grew to 140 feet (43 m) long. *Argentinosaurus* lived about 100 million years ago. It was probably hunted by packs of *Mapusaurus*, the largest known meat eater. Scientists working in Patagonia found one of the earliest known dinosaurs in 1993. Called *Eoraptor*, this dog-sized dinosaur lived about 230 million years ago.

In 1998, scientists found a field with hundreds of fossilized dinosaur eggs in Auca Mahuida, in a remote corner of northwestern Patagonia. They were eggs from the *Sauropod*, a plant-eating dinosaur. Some of the eggs even contained fossilized embryos, tiny developing dinosaurs.

Megellanic penguins breed on the Valdés Peninsula and on islands off the Argentine coast. After the chicks are able to take care of themselves, many of the penguins migrate north to Brazil.

In the Skies

More than a thousand species of birds can be found in Argentina. They range from penguins to colorful parrots and toucans to the condor, one of the largest birds in the world. The Andean condor flies throughout the western portion of Argentina. The wingspan of the male Andean condor can reach more than 10 feet (3 m).

Argentina's national bird is one of the least noticeable—the little brown ovenbird. The ovenbird uses its feet to grasp twigs and grasses, which it mixes with mud to build an oven-shaped nest on a tree branch or a fence post. By the time eggs hatch, the nest is almost completely enclosed. The warmth in the enclosed nests makes ovenbird eggs hatch more quickly than many other bird eggs.

Halfway between Buenos Aires and Tierra del Fuego is the Valdés Peninsula, which is famous for its wildlife. The peninsula

The Amazing Flyer

A small shorebird called the golden plover is a champion flier. It breeds in northern Canada. As summer comes to an end, the plovers gather in northeastern Canada. Then they head out over the Atlantic Ocean, flying nonstop to the coast of South America. Traveling at up to 60 miles per hour (100 kph), they make this 3,000-mile (5,000 km) trip in just two or three days. After resting and feeding for a few days, the birds continue south to Patagonia. In all, golden plovers migrate about 20,000 miles (32,000 km) a year!

is home to many kinds of birds, including petrels, cormorants, and albatrosses. Several million flightless Magellanic penguins live in a protected colony on the Valdés Peninsula.

Rheas, large birds that look like ostriches, can be seen running across the open grasslands of Argentina. Two types of rheas live in Argentina, one in the dry scrublands of Patagonia, the other in the Pampas. In Patagonia, they are often welcome among herds of sheep because they eat seeds that would otherwise get into the sheep's wool. Farmers, however, sometimes kill the birds, because rheas will eat almost any crop. After females lay eggs, the males sit on the eggs to keep them warm. The males also take care of the young, charging any creature that gets near them.

Horses, Cattle, and More

In the years after Europeans began settling in Argentina, the Pampas became known for its wild horses. These horses were descended from horses abandoned by early Spanish settlers. The animals flourished in the wild, becoming great herds that roamed free across the grasslands. Indigenous people caught the animals and became riders. Later, some of them—the famous

Llamas make good pack animals. They can carry loads of up to about 130 pounds (60 kg).

gauchos—turned these animals into workhorses on the Pampas. Gauchos carried out all their daily activities from the back of their mounts.

The drier regions of Argentina are home to four relatives of the camel—the llama, the guanaco, the vicuña, and the alpaca. The llama and the smaller alpaca are domesticated mammals that indigenous people use for transport, wool, and meat. The guanaco and the vicuña are wild. The guanaco lives on the plains of Patagonia. The much smaller vicuña lives in the higher mountains, where it has become threatened by overhunting for its ultrasoft fur.

Patagonia is home to sheep—millions of them. These grass-nibbling animals are slowly destroying the grassy areas of the south. Unlike cattle, sheep bite down to the roots of grass plants. As the plants die off, the soil is left exposed and wind blows it away. Perhaps 80 percent of Patagonia is in danger of turning into desert.

Trees

Much of Argentina is arid and does not have a huge variety of trees. Most of the nation's trees grow in the rain forests of the north. Argentines are trying to preserve some kinds of trees that are threatened by development. Yatay palm trees are preserved in El Palmar National Park in Entre Ríos province. Many of these trees are eight hundred years old. The myrtle wood tree is protected in Los Arrayanes National Park. It has smooth, reddish-brown bark with white spots.

El Rey National Park near Salta preserves some amazing cloud forests. Cloud forests are a type of forest that grows on mountains that are almost always covered in mist. Orchids, vines, and mosses are common in cloud forests. So are bromeliads, which grow on the branches of trees rather than in the soil. Like many plants in the cloud forest, bromeliads get their moisture and nutrients from rain and the air, rather than from the soil.

Ombú trees do not require much water, so they thrive on the Pampas. They often have several trunks, which means they are actually large evergreen bushes rather than trees. Ombús can measure as far around as they are tall, 40 to 50 feet (12 to 15 m). They are tall enough to stand out like beacons across the flat plains.

Ombús are the only treelike plant on the Pampas. The trunk of an ombú can store a lot of water, allowing it to survive in the dry region.

A Challenge to Monkeys

Monkey-puzzle trees have been planted in gardens throughout the world, but their natural habitat is a narrow band among the lakes by the Andes. This type of tree gets its name from the complicated intertwining structure of the branches, an arrangement that supposedly would puzzle a monkey trying to climb them. The species' original Mapuche name *pehuén* is now more widely used. Many of Argentina's trees are protected.

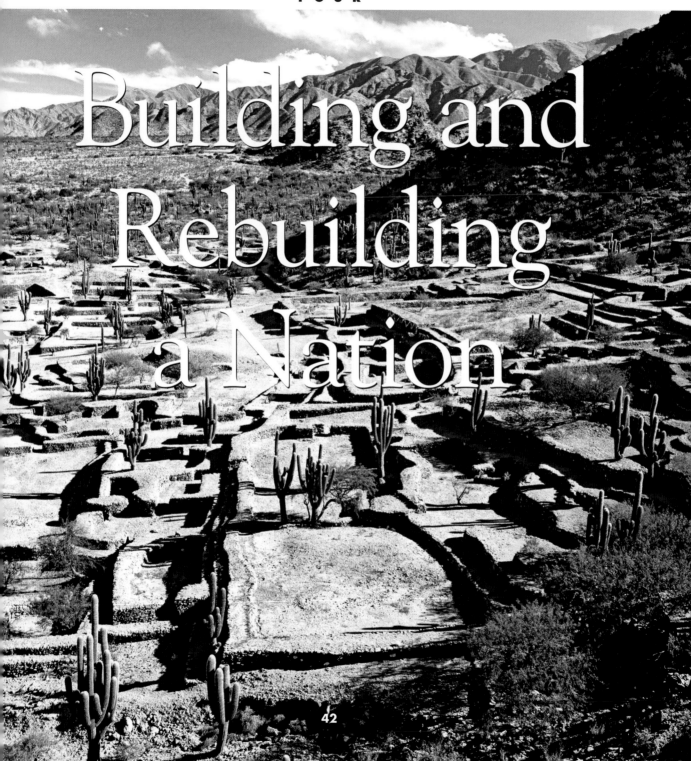

Building and Rebuilding a Nation

THE FIRST HUMANS ENTERED SOUTH AMERICA FIFTEEN thousand to twenty thousand years ago. By about seven thousand years ago, long-term settlements, where indigenous people farmed, were being created. In the land that would become Argentina, these settlements were mostly in the north, where there was enough water to support crops.

Several different indigenous cultures had developed by the time the Spaniards first arrived in the 1500s. Probably the largest native group was the Guaraní. The Guaraní lived in villages and farmed the surrounding area. Growing crops on the same land year after year would use up the nutrients in the soil. Then their crops would no longer grow well, so

Opposite: **The Quilmes people had lived in what is now northwestern Argentina since the 800s. The Spaniards destroyed their settlement and forced them to move in the 1600s.**

The Cave of the Hands

Among the oldest evidence of the ancient people who occupied Argentina is the Cave of the Hands. Paintings on the cave walls date from 9,370 years ago. Most of the paintings are of hands, and most of the hands are left hands! The cave is located in the western part of Patagonia.

the Guaraní would move on to a new area. Elsewhere in Argentina, people were nomads, moving from place to place to hunt and gather food. But the lives of the indigenous people would change forever when a new people arrived.

Exploration and Founding Settlements

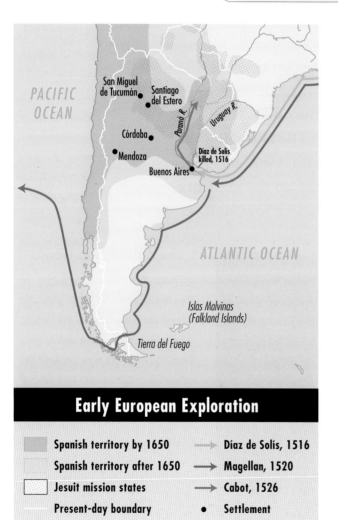

Early European Exploration

▨ Spanish territory by 1650	→ Díaz de Solís, 1516
▧ Spanish territory after 1650	→ Magellan, 1520
▢ Jesuit mission states	→ Cabot, 1526
— Present-day boundary	● Settlement

The search for a northwest passage— a water route from the Atlantic to the Pacific ocean—led European explorers to venture into North America in the years following Christopher Columbus's first journey to the Western Hemisphere in 1492. The same thing happened in South America when Juan Díaz de Solís sought a southwest passage to Asia in 1516. Instead, he discovered a wide estuary, the mouth of the Río de la Plata, and claimed the lands around it for Spain. He and some men landed briefly, but they were scared back to the ship by a group of indigenous people. Solís himself was killed during the skirmish. Some sailors grabbed up silver pieces while ashore. These pieces fed a rumor in Spain that there was a "mountain of silver" in Argentina.

Ferdinand Magellan sailed to the Río de la Plata when he was leading the first journey around the world. He reached the big estuary in 1520 and explored it. Later that same year, he found a route between the mainland and the islands of Tierra del Fuego. That passage is now called the Strait of Magellan.

In 1526, another explorer, Sebastian Cabot, traveled up the rivers that form the estuary. During that adventure, some indigenous people gave him silver pieces, and he named the estuary Río de la Plata, or "River of Silver."

None of these early explorers planned to stay. But the next expedition would be different. In 1536, Pedro de Mendoza led a party of two thousand people to Argentina. They founded Buenos Aires on the south shore of the Río de La Plata. The local indigenous people raided the settlement, trying to force the newcomers away. The settlement was quickly abandoned.

Buenos Aires was founded a second time in the same location in 1580 by troops under Juan de Garay. Only three hundred people lived in the settlement, but this time the

Above left: **Ferdinand Magellan is often called the first person to sail around the world, but he himself did not complete the trip. He was killed halfway through the three-year voyage, and his crew continued on without him.**

Above right: **Sebastian Cabot was attempting a trip around the world when he explored Argentina. A lack of food and quarrels with his crew forced him to return to Europe.**

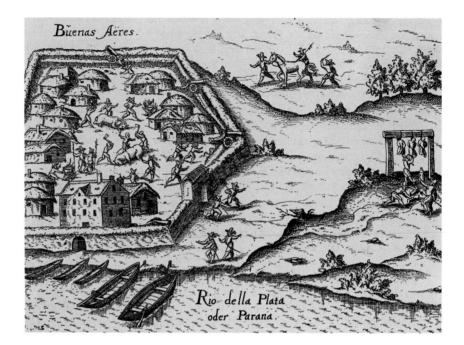

Buenos Aires began as a tiny settlement in the 1500s. Fights between the Spaniards and the indigenous people were common.

city took hold. One reason for its success may have been that pirates soon discovered it was a good place to hide from Spanish officials.

Between the two foundings of Buenos Aires, several other Argentine cities were founded. After Spanish *conquistadores*, or conquerors, defeated the Inca Empire in Peru, some of the soldiers moved south into Argentina. The first city they founded was Santiago del Estero in 1553. Soon, Mendoza, Tucumán, and Córdoba were also begun.

The Early Years

Roman Catholic priests arrived in the northern Argentina region in 1585 to try to convert the native people to Christianity. They established missions, where the native people lived, worked, and learned about the Catholic religion. The missionary priests eventually controlled the lives of the people in the surrounding regions, and the missions grew into small cities.

The Spaniards who settled Argentina brought cattle with them. They let the cattle roam free on the vast grasslands of the Pampas. The cattle eventually pushed out the animals that the indigenous people had traditionally hunted. Since the native people no longer had their traditional food sources, they began stealing cattle and horses. European settlers came to regard the native people as dangerous. As a result, many indigenous people in Argentina were killed.

In the early 1700s, slave ships from Africa began to appear at Buenos Aires. Spain and Britain agreed that the British would be the only slave dealers in Argentina. Most Argentine slaves were sent to other countries.

In 1776, the Spanish king created a huge province called the Viceroyalty of Río de la Plata. This new province included what is now Argentina, Uruguay, Paraguay, and

Viceroyalty of Río de la Plata (1776–1810)

Viceroyalty of Río de la Plata

• Settlement

PERU Modern country

—— Present-day boundary

northern Chile. Buenos Aires became the capital of the province. However, Spain showed little interest in its new colony because the land had neither precious metals nor spices. It was regarded as a large, empty space attached to Peru. At the beginning of the nineteenth century, the attention of Spain turned toward Europe as Napoléon Bonaparte of France tried to take over country after country. The people in Argentina were left to fend for themselves.

It was already clear that the Pampas was a great place to raise cattle and horses. People began claiming vast sections of land. Raising cattle became a commercial business.

Buenos Aires grew into a large city with an economy based on trade. It became the capital of the sprawling Viceroyalty of Río de la Plata in 1776.

British troops invaded
Buenos Aires twice in the
early 1800s. Local militias
fought them off.

Some indigenous men decided to work on these ranches.
They became the gauchos, and the new landowners became
the political powers who would control Argentina for decades
to come.

Approaching Independence

In 1806, British troops invaded Buenos Aires. They hoped
to steal Argentina from Spanish control while the Spaniards
were focused on events in Europe. But the Argentines managed to throw out the British troops without help from Spain.
The following year, the same thing happened. These successes
encouraged the Argentines to seek independence.

On May 25, 1810, the leaders of Buenos Aires declared
that they no longer owed allegiance to Spain. They made this
statement after Napoléon's troops invaded Spain. At the time,
the Argentine leaders declared they still owed allegiance to
the Spanish king himself. Then, on July 9, 1816, Argentina
declared itself completely independent.

The Liberator

José de San Martín (1778–1850) was the father of Argentine independence. He was born in Yapeyú in the province of Corrientes. He grew up in Spain and served in the army there, fighting Napoléon's troops. In time, he came to oppose Spanish rule. He went to Argentina in 1812 and took charge of an army of revolutionaries that liberated the Río de la Plata region from Spain. In 1816, he was the major influence behind Argentina's declaration of independence. He then led his army on a terrible journey across the peaks of the Andes to Chile and then north into Peru. He helped both those countries become independent nations. "The Liberator" refused to remain a public figure. In 1824, he sailed to France, where he lived out his life. From afar, he watched as the land he liberated fell into war.

a prefirió mas que la
rtad de su Patria.

Wars Large and Small

After Argentina became independent, a civil war erupted between two groups—the Unitarists and the Federalists. It was the same kind of disagreement that erupted when the United States was being formed. Some people—in this case the Unitarists—wanted a strong central government. The others, the Federalists, were landowners who wanted the different regions to have their own strong governments, with a weak central government. In 1829, Federalist troops under Juan Manuel de Rosas took control of Buenos Aires.

Many people were loyal to Rosas because he provided work and security. The landowners were loyal because he allowed them to claim huge stretches of land in the Pampas. But Rosas was a cruel dictator. He was overthrown in 1852 by an army led by

Justo José de Urquiza. Urquiza put together a legislature, which drew up Argentina's first constitution. He became president of the new organization of provinces, called a confederation. But Buenos Aires refused to follow the lead of the provinces, and the provinces rejected leadership by the city. Finally, in 1862, a new national government with a new president was formed.

From 1864 to 1870, Brazil, Argentina, and Uruguay combined forces against Paraguay, which was trying to acquire land that would give it a port. What followed was the War of the Triple Alliance, the bloodiest war in Latin American history. As many as one million people died, including more than half of Paraguay's population—almost all the able-bodied Guaraní men.

The Conquest of the Desert

The European Argentines paid little attention to what happened south of Buenos Aires. They left these areas to the native people. But, as in earlier years, the indigenous people sometimes stole cattle. Finally, white troops entered these areas to try to punish the native people. Gradually, European influence spread throughout the distant Pampas and Patagonia.

European Argentines came to believe that the "Desert"— meaning the Pampas, Patagonia, and Tierra del Fuego—had to be colonized. General Julio A. Roca, who was president from 1880 to 1886 and again some years later, led this twenty-five-year effort. It became known as the Conquest of the Desert. The Europeans of Buenos Aires took over the Desert, and the indigenous people became second-class citizens.

Cattle ranching was important in Argentina, and the great landowners became the most important people in the nation. The landowners governed because of what was known as "the Agreement." Several political parties agreed that land and business were more important than politics. They agreed that they would take turns governing but never really change anything. Certainly, they would never let a political party that might upset their way of life take over. The Agreement continued until 1912, when the public protested government corruption. Finally, some reforms were made. All adult men could now vote by secret ballot. In 1916, Hipólito Yrigoyen was elected president. He was the first leader in South America chosen in an election in which all men could vote.

In the late 1800s, European immigrants began settling in parts of Argentina where before only indigenous people had lived.

Many people expected Argentina to become the model for all Latin American nations. It would be the southern balance to the United States. Argentina's economy flourished as its farm products were shipped to markets across Europe. New immigrants poured into the country. More than three million Europeans arrived between 1875 and 1914. Buenos Aires was on its way to becoming a "European" city. In the coming years, grand streets were laid out and large buildings were erected. Argentina had become one of the world's wealthiest nations, and Buenos Aires was the pride of Latin America.

Again No Democracy

In 1929, a severe economic slump called the Great Depression began in the United States. Nations around the world, including Argentina, suffered. The following year, General José Félix Uriburu overthrew Yrigoyen, who had again been elected president. This was the first time Argentina's military had ousted a democratically elected leader. Uriburu outlawed political parties that opposed his dictatorship. Several political parties joined forces to retain control of the Argentine government for the next twelve years. They rigged elections to make their parties look popular. When the economy improved, the government got the credit.

Juan Perón waves to the crowd at a parade following his first inauguration, in 1946.

In time, civilians were again elected Argentina's leaders. But then, in 1943, the military again overthrew the civilian government. This opened the way for the dictatorship of Colonel Juan Domingo Perón.

The Perón Years

Juan Perón gained power through the military. He became vice president after the military took over Argentina. In 1946, having become popular with working people, he was elected president. Perón and his second wife, Eva Duarte, were given credit when health services and pensions were created for the people.

Evita—Lady of Hope

María Eva Duarte was born in 1919 in the poor village of Los Toldos. Her mother had spent fifteen years in a relationship with a married man, Juan Duarte. After his death, his children had to work as servants in the homes of the wealthy. Eva understood well the difference between rich and poor.

In 1934, Eva went to Buenos Aires, where she became a popular performer on radio soap operas. At a party in 1944, she met an army colonel, Juan Domingo Perón. She married him the following year. He was campaigning to be president of Argentina, and Eva helped make him popular. Known as the "Lady of Hope," she worked to gain women the right to vote.

Eva Duarte de Perón died of cancer in 1952 at age thirty-three. Her husband's cruelties soon turned the people against him, and he was forced to flee the

country. Twenty years later, Juan Perón again came to power in Argentina. He then had his beloved wife's body, which had been buried in Italy, returned to Buenos Aires for burial.

Under Perón, more Argentines took part in the political process. He frequently called for public gatherings that, for the first time, let workers and poor people—whom he called "the shirtless"—gather in downtown Buenos Aires. Both he and Eva spoke to the people with inspiring words. Eva became known by the affectionate nickname Evita.

Perón changed the constitution so that he could serve a second term as president. He was becoming increasingly dictatorial. He controlled what was said in schools, he shut down newspapers, and he jailed his opponents. His supporters withdrew their support. On June 16, 1955, naval and air force officers bombed the government palace, hoping to kill Perón.

Instead, about three hundred people outside in the plaza were killed. Three months later, the military seized power, and Perón fled the country.

In the following years, Argentina's economy spun out of control. Soon, many people could no longer afford to feed themselves. The 1970s was a period of riots in the cities. The riots were in response to the harsh practices of a new dictator, General Juan Carlos Onganía. Some groups began demanding that Juan Perón return. One group, the Montoneros, carried out kidnappings and assassinations to shake up the people in power.

In March 1973, an election was held for the first time in ten years. Héctor Cámpora, a supporter of Perón, was elected president. A few months later, he quit so that Perón could return to Argentina and take over the presidency. Perón's third wife, Isabel Martínez de Perón, became the vice president. Juan Perón died in July 1974. His wife was sworn in as president, but she was unable to control the many factions in Argentina. The military took over again on March 24, 1976.

The Dirty War

A small group of military officers, called a junta, established a new government. The junta dissolved the National Congress. They ruled by terror. During the seven years the junta was in control, thousands of people were jailed and tortured. The military leaders claimed that violence was necessary to keep the country stable. Some opponents quietly disappeared, and their graves have never been found. This period is called the Dirty

The Mothers of Plaza de Mayo

Young people, artists, writers, and journalists were among the many thousands who disappeared during the junta's rule. When no one did anything, their mothers began to protest. Despite the danger, many women began to gather in Plaza de Mayo every Thursday.

When grandmothers, too, began appearing in the plaza, the women were able to get attention from foreign newspapers and human rights workers. Even the junta leaders could not take public action against grieving mothers and grandmothers without an international outcry. Instead, they tried to convince the public that the women were insane. Some of the mothers, like their children, disappeared. Finally, in 2006, the mothers agreed that the new government cared about the disappeareds and would investigate. Now they march for other causes.

War. The many missing people are called "the disappeareds," *los desaparecidos* in Spanish. It is estimated that as many as thirty thousand people disappeared during the junta's rule.

The Falklands War

By 1982, the Argentine economy was failing and the military dictatorship was weakening. Public protests began as the economy continued to slide. In March, labor unions organized a large nationwide strike. The police brutally put down the strikers, causing more public protest. Hoping to regain public trust, the junta announced that troops had invaded the Falkland Islands to reclaim them from the British.

The islands, called *Islas Malvinas* in Spanish, are located about 300 miles (500 km) off the coast of southern Argentina. They had been occupied by Britian since 1833. Many Argentines believed that Argentina should own the islands because the islands were nearby and had once been ruled by Spain. They were delighted that their country had retaken the islands.

What they didn't expect was that Britain would go to war to hold on to the islands. It took seven weeks for British troops

British troops in action during the Falklands War. The war lasted seventy-four days and caused nearly a thousand deaths.

to arrive in the Falklands. When they did, unprepared Argentine troops quickly lost. More than 630 Argentine soldiers died. This loss caused the collapse of the military dictatorship. A genuine democratic election was held in 1983, and Raúl Alfonsín was elected president.

The Years Since

Alfonsín created a commission to investigate the thousands of disappeareds. But few junta members were tried for the crimes because other former military leaders demanded that the trials stop. Alfonsín was afraid that the military would again take over the country if he did not agree to stop the investigation. Laws were passed preventing any more trials of senior officers.

Alfonsín also faced a huge debt that had developed under the military dictatorship. Because of that debt, prices rose rapidly. Suddenly, millions of Argentines could no longer pay their rent or even buy food. Alfonsín was forced to resign and a new election was held.

Carlos Saúl Menem was elected president. Menem managed to control prices and stabilize Argentina's economy. But people in rural areas faced deepening poverty. City slums also expanded. Menem dominated Argentina from 1989 until he was forced to leave office in 1999. Two years later, the corruption of his government became known, and, facing arrest, Menem fled to Peru.

Menem was followed by Fernando de la Rúa. In 2001, Argentina faced another economic crisis. Money began flowing out of the country to foreign banks and investments. To stop this, de la Rúa limited the amount of money that people could withdraw from their bank accounts. The result was widespread protests in which twenty-eight people were killed. De la Rúa was forced from office.

The next month saw three presidents come and go before one finally managed to hold on to the office. Under the new government led by Eduardo Duhalde, the economic crisis continued. The value of the Argentine peso dropped suddenly. Argentines' money was now worth next to nothing.

Raúl Alfonsín (left) shakes hands with Carlos Saúl Menem, who followed him as president. The two held office during a time of economic upheaval.

Businesses failed, driving unemployment up. Finally, in late 2002, the economy stabilized.

In 2003, Néstor Kirchner was elected president. Early in his term, Kirchner replaced judges on the Argentine Supreme Court who had been loyal to Menem. In 2005, the new Supreme Court struck down the laws that had prevented trials of the military leaders who had been responsible for the disappeareds. Finally, after more than twenty years, charges against them could be made. The first trial began in 2006.

For nearly a century, Argentine history has been a mix of democracy, military takeovers, and economic turmoil. Any one of these three elements may rise to the top at any time. Perhaps, though, democracy will become the dominant reality for the Argentine people.

The Changeable Government

ARGENTINA IS DIVIDED INTO TWENTY-THREE PRO-
vinces, which are like U.S. states, and a federal district, which
is like Washington, D.C. The federal district is the core
of Buenos Aires, the nation's capital. Almost one-third of
Argentines live in the metropolitan area of Buenos Aires.

Opposite: **The Cabildo in Buenos Aires housed the government in colonial times. Now it is a museum.**

The Constitution

Argentina's constitution was adopted in 1853 and changed in
1994. It was based to a large extent on the U.S. Constitution.
It makes Argentina a federal democracy. That means the different parts of the country—the provinces—have agreed to
give up certain powers to a
central government.

Argentina's military ousted the government in 1943. The military domi-nated Argentina for much of the twentieth century.

Argentine leaders have
often found it easy to ignore
the constitution. During
one fifty-year period in the
twentieth century, only three
democratic presidential elections were held. Whenever a
government was considered
weak—usually as a result of
a weak economy—it was ripe
for takeover by the military
or a dictator.

The Constitution and Indigenous Peoples

The Argentine Constitution was changed in 1994. Among the changes was the new Law of Indigenous Rights. For the first time in history, the Argentine government acknowledged the rights of indigenous peoples. Originally, the constitution said that the government had the goal of converting indigenous peoples to Catholicism. That was removed from the constitution in 1994.

The National Government

Argentina's government is divided into three branches: executive, legislative, and judicial. All citizens at least eighteen years old are required to vote.

The head of the executive branch is the president. Both the president and the vice president are elected by the people to four-year terms. They may serve two terms in a row. The various departments of the executive branch are run by the cabinet ministers appointed by the president.

President Domingo Fausto Sarmiento nicknamed the presidential palace "Casa Rosada" in 1873. It means "Pink House."

Working for Peace

Two Argentines have been awarded the Nobel Peace Prize. In 1936, this honor went to Carlos Saavedra Lamas (1878–1959). As Argentina's foreign minister, he helped end the Chaco War between Paraguay and Bolivia. He later served as president of the League of Nations. Like today's United Nations, the League of Nations was an international organization committed to settling conflicts between nations peacefully. In 1980, Adolfo Pérez Esquivel (1931–) won the Nobel Peace Prize for his work in human rights in Argentina. Though trained as a sculptor and architect, he gave up that work to help organize nonviolent groups in Latin America. He also helped persuade the United Nations to establish its Human Rights Commission.

The legislative branch, the National Congress, is made up of two houses. Members of the upper house, or Senate, are elected by the residents of the various provinces. The Senate has seventy-two seats, with each of the twenty-three provinces plus the federal district electing three senators. Two of those senators must represent the major political party in the province. The third must come from the second-largest political party. One-third of all senators come up for election every two years.

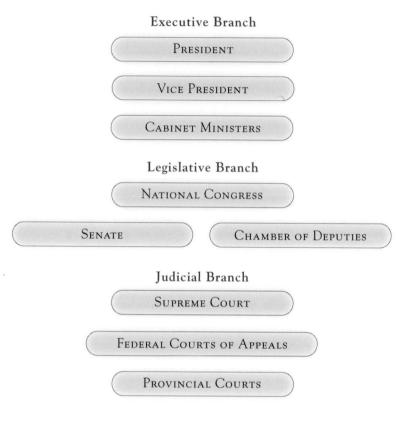

NATIONAL GOVERNMENT OF ARGENTINA

Executive Branch

PRESIDENT

VICE PRESIDENT

CABINET MINISTERS

Legislative Branch

NATIONAL CONGRESS

SENATE

CHAMBER OF DEPUTIES

Judicial Branch

SUPREME COURT

FEDERAL COURTS OF APPEALS

PROVINCIAL COURTS

The lower house is the Chamber of Deputies. It has 257 seats. Deputies serve four-year terms, with one-half of the seats up for election every two years. At least 30 percent of the representatives to congress are supposed to be women.

Argentina's judicial branch is headed by the Supreme Court, which has nine judges. They are appointed by the president, but the appointments must be approved by at least two-thirds of the Senate. The judges in lower courts are appointed by the president. The Federal Courts of Appeals deal with cases that have a national impact. Provincial courts deal with cases of local interest.

Political Parties

Argentina's two main political parties are the Justicialist Party and the Radical Civic Union. The Justicialist Party generally supports the policies of former president Juan Perón, such as heavy government spending. Traditionally, laborers have backed the Justicialist Party. The Radical Civic Union draws more support from the middle class. In recent years, the traditional lines between the parties have been breaking down, and smaller parties have been gaining support. Néstor Kirchner, who was elected president of Argentina in 2003, belongs to the Justicialist Party.

President Néstor Kirchner gives a speech in the Casa Rosada.

The Flag

The Argentine flag has three equal horizontal bands, light blue on the top and bottom and white in between. On the center of the white band is the Sun of May, a radiant yellow sun with a human face. Argentines celebrate Flag Day on June 20, the day on which the designer of Argentina's flag, Manuel Belgrano, died.

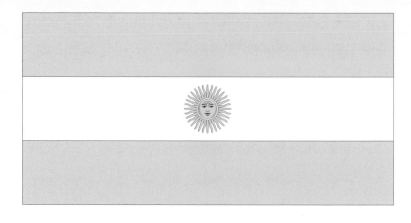

The Military

The Argentine military consists of the army, navy, and air force. They are part of the Ministry of Defense. The Ministry of the Interior oversees the border police and the coast guard. Military service is voluntary, and currently the nation has fewer than seventy-five thousand troops.

National Symbols

The national flower is actually a tree, the ceibo. It has clusters of gorgeous red blossoms. The national stone is Inca rose, or rhodochrosite, a pink stone with white streaks. The national animal is the ovenbird. Its name comes from the shape of its nest.

The National Anthem

The national anthem of Argentina is *"!Oid, Mortales!"* ("Hear, O Mortals!"). It was adopted in 1813 and updated in 1924. The words are by Vincente López y Planes and the music is by José Blas Parera.

Spanish Lyrics

¡Oíd mortales! el grito sagrado:
¡Libertad, Libertad, Libertad!
Oíd el ruido de rotas cadenas:
Ved en trono a la noble Igualdad.
¡Ya su trono dignísimo abrieron
Las provincias unidas del Sud!
Y los libres del mundo responden:
¡Al Gran Pueblo Argentino Salud!
¡Al Gran Pueblo Argentino Salud!
Y los libres del mundo responden:
¡Al Gran Pueblo Argentino Salud!
Y los libres del mundo responden:
¡Al Gran Pueblo Argentino Salud!
CHORUS
Sean eternos los laureles
Que supimos conseguir.
Coronados de gloria vivamos
O juremos con gloria morir.
(repeat three times)

English Lyrics

Mortals! Hear the sacred cry;
Freedom! Freedom! Freedom!
Hear the noise of broken chains.
See noble Equality enthroned.
The United Provinces of the South
Have now displayed their worthy throne.
And the free peoples of the world reply;
We salute the great people of Argentina!
We salute the great people of Argentina!
And the free peoples of the world reply;
We salute the great people of Argentina!
And the free peoples of the world reply;
We salute the great people of Argentina!
CHORUS
May the laurels be eternal
That we knew how to win.
Let us live crowned with glory,
Or swear to die gloriously.
(repeat three times)

In Argentina's history, the military has frequently overthrown democratically elected governments. Since 1983, the military has pledged to respect the democratic institutions of the country. Perhaps the days of military dictatorships in Argentina are past.

Buenos Aires: Did You Know This?

Buenos Aires, the capital of Argentina, is the second-largest city in South America, with a population of 11,600,000. People born in Buenos Aires call themselves *porteños* ("people of the port"), indicating that their ancestors arrived in Argentina from Europe through the city's port. The port, located on the Río de la Plata, is one of the busiest in the world.

Plaza de Mayo (above) is the heart of the old part of the city. On the east side of the plaza is the pink presidential palace, called Casa Rosada, ("Pink House"). Political rallies and protests are often held in front of that building. The huge Metropolitan Cathedral is also located on the plaza. The Argentine hero General José de San Martín is buried there. Another building on the plaza is the Cabildo, the City Council chambers used when Spain ruled the area. The Argentine declaration of independence was signed within its old walls. In the middle of the plaza is a soaring monument. It was built in 1811 to commemorate the first anniversary of Argentine independence.

On Avenida Nueve de Julio stands a tall tower that looks like the Washington Monument in Washington,

D.C. Built in 1936 to mark the four hundredth anniversary of the founding of the city, it stands 220 feet (67 m) high. The English Tower is another famous tower in Buenos Aires. It looks like the tower in London that holds the clock called Big Ben. The English Tower's chimes ring out over the city every hour.

No cars are allowed on two main streets downtown. Instead, people walk from store to store. Shopping is also fun at San Telmo Fair, an open-air market held every Sunday in Plaza Dorrego. It specializes in antiques.

Bright buses travel through downtown Buenos Aires, while subway trains rumble under the streets. Built in 1912, the city's subway system is one of the oldest in the world. The stations are decorated with colorful tile murals. The neighborhood called La Boca also features exuberant colors. The trend to paint houses in purples, greens, and reds was started by immigrants from Genoa, Italy, who settled the area.

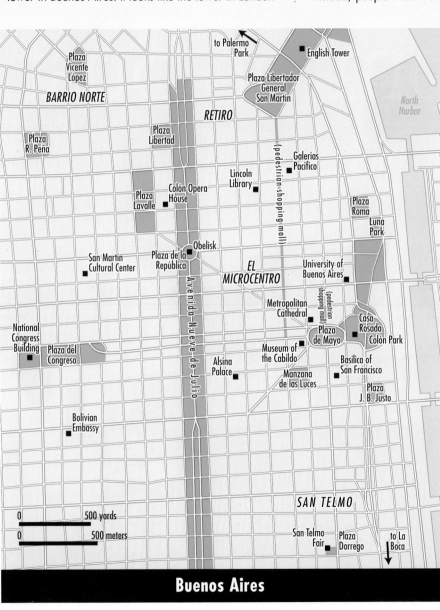

Buenos Aires

Boom or Bust

At times during its history, Argentina has been a very wealthy nation. It had the highest income per person in Latin America in 1929, at the start of the worldwide Great Depression. After the Depression, it was again in good shape. But then, in the 1970s, things began to change rapidly. Dictators halted the nation's political advances and put policies in place that hurt the nation's economy. Not only did the people have to endure a bloody dictatorship, they were left with a worse standard of living and a nation severely in debt.

Opposite: **Many Argentines were awash in money in the 1920s. This magnificent house was built for the son of a cattle rancher.**

Money Facts

Argentina's currency is the Argentine peso, which is divided into one hundred centavos. In 2006, one U.S. dollar equaled about three pesos. Argentine coins have values of 1, 5, 10, 25, and 50 centavos. Bills are worth 2, 5, 10, 20, 50, and 100 pesos. The bills show portraits of famous Argentines on one side. Buildings, monuments, or scenes from history grace the other side.

The Cattle Business

Spaniards brought horses and cattle to the Western Hemisphere. When they released the animals onto the Pampas, the animals thrived and multiplied. A new elite of landowning people developed. They lived on *estancias,* "estates" or "ranches," and were called the *estancieros.* Prestige came from owning vast amounts of land, so estates were rarely broken up. Newcomers to the country were unable to buy land.

Cattle ranching remains a big business in Argentina. Livestock shows in Buenos Aires attract people from all over Argentina and the world. The finest cattle and horses are shown and sold amid a great party atmosphere.

Argentines consume more beef than almost any other people on earth. In the early days of the cattle industry, the

A cowboy herds cattle in Patagonia. Argentina produces about 2.5 million tons of beef each year.

meat was kept in Argentina and eaten quickly, or it was salted to preserve it and then shipped overseas. Things changed in the late 1800s when Argentines developed ways to cool and store meat for long periods of time. They began to ship their fine beef to distant countries for the first time. Today, the main buyers of Argentine beef are the United States, Germany, and Chile.

Growing Crops and Raising Sheep

Argentines grow a great deal of grain to feed all those cattle. They also produce sunflower seeds, lemons, soybeans, grapes, corn, tobacco, peanuts, and tea. Workers from Bolivia and Chile help pick grapes, sugarcane, cotton, and tobacco in the north. Cotton is raised in the province of Chaco and sugarcane near Tucumán province. Grapes and other fruits grow around Mendoza and the province of San Juan. Argentine grapes aren't just for eating; they are also used in making wine. The country has always produced good wines, but until recently they were sold only at home. Now a great deal of Argentine wine is exported to other countries.

Most Argentine sheep farms are in Patagonia. The largest landowner in Argentina is Benetton, the huge Italian clothing

Mendoza province in the west is one of Argentina's main grape-growing regions. Argentina is the world's fifth-largest wine producer.

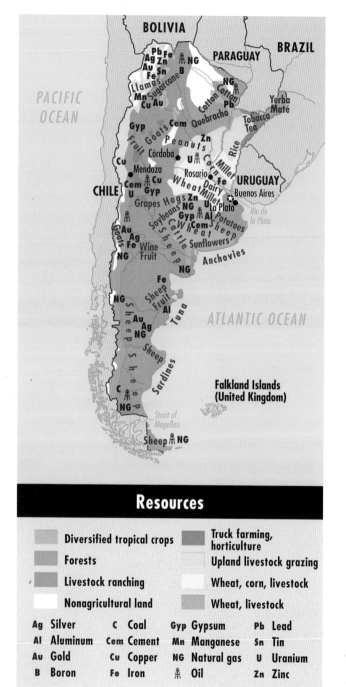

Resources

▨ Diversified tropical crops	▨ Truck farming, horticulture	
▨ Forests	▨ Upland livestock grazing	
▨ Livestock ranching	▨ Wheat, corn, livestock	
▨ Nonagricultural land	▨ Wheat, livestock	

Ag	Silver	C	Coal	Gyp	Gypsum	Pb	Lead
Al	Aluminum	Cem	Cement	Mn	Manganese	Sn	Tin
Au	Gold	Cu	Copper	NG	Natural gas	U	Uranium
B	Boron	Fe	Iron	⛏	Oil	Zn	Zinc

maker. It owns 2.2 million acres (900,000 hectares) in Patagonia. The company raises 280,000 sheep there, which produce about 10 percent of the wool Benetton needs.

Mineral Resources

Argentina has many valuable minerals beneath the ground, but only in recent years have they begun to be explored and mined. The country's mineral resources include lead, zinc, tin, copper, gold, iron ore, manganese, aluminum, uranium, and petroleum. Most of the minerals are located along the edge of the Andes Mountains.

The Patagonian province of Santa Cruz is rich in oil. The region produces so much oil that Argentina does not need to import any. Interestingly, the Santa Cruz area itself relies heavily on wind energy instead of oil. Argentina is also a large producer of natural gas. About 17 percent of the country's natural gas is exported to surrounding countries. The rest is used to meet about half of the nation's electricity needs.

What Argentina Grows, Makes, and Mines

Agriculture (2003)

Soybeans	34,800,000 metric tons
Sugarcane	19,250,000 metric tons
Corn	15,040,000 metric tons

Manufacturing (2005)

Processed oil	33,560,700 cubic meters
Motor Vehicles	320,000 units

Mining (2003)

Oil	270,340,000 barrels
Natural gas	50,664 million cubic meters
Silver	133,917 kilograms

Nearly two hundred thousand cars are made in Argentina each year.

Manufacturing

Manufacturing is a big part of the Argentine economy. In fact, Argentina's factories are so active that the country does not need to import consumer goods. Argentina has been making cars since the 1920s. Fiat maintains a huge plant at Córdoba. Ford, General Motors, Toyota, and Volkswagen also make cars in Argentina. Many cars are made for export.

Argentina also makes auto parts, many kinds of plastics, leather goods, and computer software. It exports steel, turbines for power plants, and platforms for offshore drilling.

The first newspaper to be published in Buenos Aires began on June 7, 1810. The main newspapers published today are *La Prenza* and *La Nación*. Both began publishing in about 1870. Radio began about 1920, and television in the late 1950s. Although a few of the stations are owned by the national and provincial governments, most are privately owned. Venezuela and Argentina are joining forces on some state-owned TV channels.

The Internet quickly became popular in Argentina. At the beginning of 2006, an estimated ten million Argentines were Internet users. That is more than one-fourth of the country's population.

Internet cafés are popular in Argentina. Buenos Aires alone has about nine thousand.

Buenos Aires boasts the world's widest street. Avenida 9 de Julio has sixteen lanes of traffic.

Transportation

A higher percentage of people have cars in Argentina than in any other Latin American country. Most Argentines use their cars to commute to work. In Buenos Aires, that means heavy traffic on the streets and highways. Many drivers pay little attention to driving laws. They are certain that they know what is best . . . for them! The expressways around the cities are privately owned, so people must pay a toll to drive on them. Beyond the cities, only about one-fourth of the roads are paved.

An extensive network of buses connects Buenos Aires with smaller cities and towns. Outside the cities, bus drivers sometimes carry messages, mail, and even grocery orders.

The Steam Train

The Old Patagonian Express is a narrow-gauge rail line that pulls tourists by steam engine across Patagonia. Called *La Trochita*, the antique train runs for six and a half hours through the foothills of the Andes. Author Paul Theroux made the train famous in his book *The Old Patagonian Express: By Train Through the Americas.*

Argentina's railroad system was started in about 1865. Oddly, it failed to bring the various regions of the country together. Rail lines were built from Buenos Aires to each section of the country, but they did not connect the different sections of the country to each other. This increased the importance and growth of Buenos Aires. Today, Argentina has about 22,000 miles (35,000 km) of railway track.

Aerolíneas Argentinas is Argentina's national airline. It provides about 40 percent of the flights between Argentina and other countries and the vast majority of flights within Argentina. The main international airport, Ezeiza, is near Buenos Aires. Jorge Newberry Airport, also in Buenos Aires, is the main airport for flights within Argentina. Because Argentina is such a large country, air travel is becoming more common. The nation now has 142 airports with paved runways.

Argentina, Brazil, Uruguay, and Paraguay belong to a trade organization called Mercosur, which was founded in 1991. Its name comes from Mercado Común del Sur, meaning "Trade Community of the South." Its purpose is to promote free trade among its member nations. Countries with free-trade agreements do not tax goods imported from each other.

The Revolutionary

Ernesto Guevara Lynch de la Serna, popularly known as Che Guevara, was born in Rosario, Santa Fe, in 1928. He came from a wealthy family. Unlike many members of the elite, Che Guevara was very aware of the social differences among Argentines. After finishing medical school, he rode a motorcycle around South America for eight months. During this trip, he came to believe that the poor people of the earth could be helped only through communism. Under communism, the government controls the economy and owns most of the businesses.

In 1959, Guevara helped Fidel Castro and his communist supporters overthrow Fulgencio Batista, the dictator of Cuba, an island nation off the coast of Florida. Guevara worked with Castro for a time and then left for Bolivia, where he was killed by the army in 1967. Even though Guevara has long been dead, he has become a legend and a symbol of revolutions everywhere. His book *The Motorcycle Diaries: Notes on a Latin American Journey*, which told the tale of his trip around South America, was published in 1995 and made into a movie in 2004. The soundtrack is by Argentine composer Gustavo Santaolalla.

Venezuela became a full partner of Mercosur in 2006. Bolivia and Chile may also eventually join. Mercosur has taken a series of small steps toward eliminating trade barriers among the countries.

Economic Collapse and Recovery

When Argentina's economy collapsed in 2001, riots broke out. Banks froze accounts so people could not get at their money. The value of the peso dropped. Most people's life savings disappeared, and their income was almost useless. People who had never been without money suddenly found themselves in poverty, with little money to pay for food. One out of every five people was unemployed.

Police charge protestors in 2001. The protestors were objecting to government limits on the amount of cash they could withdraw from their bank accounts.

A homeless man and his son sit on a street in Buenos Aires. The percentage of Argentines living on less than one dollar a day dropped from 24 percent in 2002 to 12 percent in 2005.

The Argentine government could not make scheduled payments on the debt it owed other countries, a failure called a default. The nation defaulted on its $81 billion debt, the largest debt default in world history.

In 2003, Argentina's new president, Néstor Kirchner, made changes to help the country pay off its debts and get back on its economic feet. Today, Argentina's economy is improving, but it is still not stable. Unemployment had dropped to 10 percent by 2006, and continuing growth is predicted. But many Argentines are not hopeful because almost 40 percent of the people in urban areas live in poverty. For those who have jobs, though, income is rising again.

The People
of Argentina

ARGENTINA IS A LARGE AND VARIED COUNTRY. ABOUT one-third of the people live in or near Buenos Aires. Another one-third lives along the major rivers that spread out to the north. That leaves about a third sprinkled across vast lands to the south and west.

In 2005, Argentina had an estimated population of 39,537,943. About 95 percent of Argentines are of European origin, mostly Italian and Spanish. Another 4.5 percent are mestizo, people with both European and indigenous backgrounds. A tiny percentage, 5 percent, are purely indigenous.

Opposite: **Most Aregentines are of European descent.**

Ethnic Argentina

White	95%
Mestizo, indigenous, or other	5%

Buenos Aires has a European feel. It is a mix of modern skyscrapers and charming old neighborhoods.

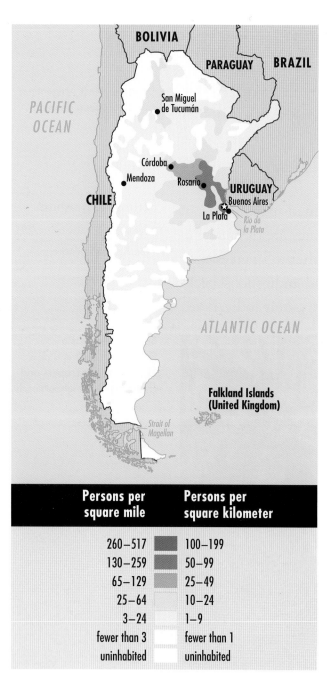

BOLIVIA

PARAGUAY   BRAZIL

PACIFIC
OCEAN

San Miguel
de Tucumán

Córdoba

Mendoza   Rosario

CHILE   URUGUAY
Buenos Aires

La Plata   Río de
la Plata

ATLANTIC OCEAN

Falkland Islands
(United Kingdom)

Strait of
Magellan

Persons per square mile		Persons per square kilometer
260–517		100–199
130–259		50–99
65–129		25–49
25–64		10–24
3–24		1–9
fewer than 3		fewer than 1
uninhabited		uninhabited

Argentines tend to be taller and blonder than people in most other Latin American countries. This is because European immigrants were less likely to have children with the native people of Argentina. Recent research has shown, however, that about 56 percent of Argentines have an indigenous ancestor in their distant past.

Indigenous Argentines

In some ways, indigenous Argentines were invisible for much of the nation's history. Many Argentines of European background ignored the fact that indigenous people had lived in Argentina first. They ignored the fact that indigenous people still lived in Argentina. After the fall of the military junta in 1983, some of the native peoples began to claim the lands their ancestors had once occupied. In 1985, President Alfonsín passed a law granting full citizenship rights to indigenous Argentines.

Experts disagree about the number of indigenous groups in Argentina.

Most groups are small, and their languages have almost died out. Language alone is not enough to reveal someone's ethnicity. This is because about four million people who speak a variety of languages moved to Argentina in the 1990s from other Latin American countries, especially Bolivia, Paraguay, and Chile. They immigrated because Argentina offered more economic opportunity than their home countries. This massive immigration means that today, more Paraguayans live in Buenos Aires than in Asunción, the capital of Paraguay.

An indigenous woman from Jujuy Province in northern Argentina carries her baby on her back. Many indigenous people live in this region.

Words from Guaraní

The Guaraní once occupied most of Paraguay and the Corrientes and Entre Ríos provinces of northeastern Argentina. Many Guaraní went to the Spanish missions that were built after 1585. The Guaraní came to the missions in large numbers because the soldiers there protected them from slave hunters.

Several Guaraní words have entered the English language. These include *jaguar* and *tapioca*. (Tapioca comes from the manioc root, which was a major part of the Guaraní diet.) In the Corrientes province, Guaraní has joined Spanish as an official government language.

Many recent immigrants speak Quechua, the primary language of northwestern Argentina. Guaraní is more common in the northeast. In Patagonia, the primary indigenous languages are Mapuche and Tehuelche.

The people who live in southern Argentina and Chile are Mapuche. Spain signed a treaty with the Mapuche in 1641, recognizing their control over much of Patagonia. In the long run, the treaty did no good. During the Conquest of the Desert from 1860 to 1885, many Mapuche were killed. The treaty was ignored.

Some indigenous groups in Argentina are suffering as the modern world intrudes on their lives. One group of Guaraní communities, called Mbya, live in Misiones province in northern Argentina. A forestry company now owns the ter-

Words from Quechua

Quechua, which is spoken in northwestern Argentina, was the language of the Inca empire in Peru. Today, it is spoken by almost ten million people in South America. This makes it the most widely spoken indigenous language in the Western Hemisphere. Quechua words that have entered English include *llama*, *pampa*, *quinine*, and *condor*. The word *gaucho* probably also comes from Quechua.

What Happened to the Slaves?

Many black slaves were brought to South America during the early nineteenth century. Though it became illegal to import slaves into Argentina in 1812, slavery itself was not outlawed until the 1853 constitution. By that time, perhaps 25 percent of Argentines were black. After slavery was outlawed, the African people gradually merged with the indigenous people, becoming part of the mestizos. For years, many people in Argentina refused to admit that some Argentines had African heritage. Only in recent years has the term *Afro-Argentine* been used.

ritory where the Mbya find food, medicine, and building materials. That company has tried to force the Mbya into an area that is only about one-twentieth of the amount of land that they need to survive.

Immigrants from Europe

Millions of immigrants poured into Argentina in the late nineteenth century and into the twentieth century. They were drawn by the country's strong economy. Not all immigrants stayed near Buenos Aires. A major German population developed on the border with Chile. Shepherds from Scotland and Ireland migrated to Patagonia. Some residents of Patagonia still speak Welsh, the language immigrants brought from Wales.

Population of Major Cities (2005 est.)

City	Population
Buenos Aires	11,600,000
Córdoba	1,450,000
Rosario	1,200,000
Mendoza	1,003,000
La Plata	810,000
Tucumán	785,000

Russians, Greeks, Poles, Lebanese, and many others came to Argentina. But the largest number of immigrants came from Italy. This fact still plays a role in Argentine life today. Much Argentine food is Italian in origin, and Italian is one of the primary spoken languages.

Pizza is popular in Argentina. It is a reminder of the many Italians who immigrated there.

The American Bandits

By 1901, there were Wanted posters all over the United States for the famous outlaws Butch Cassidy (really Robert Leroy Parker) and the Sundance Kid (Harry Longbaugh). Parker (above left) and Longbough (above right with his girlfriend, Etta Place) needed to get away, so they headed for South America. After a brief visit to Buenos Aires, they continued on to Patagonia, which they heard was similar to the American Southwest.

The two bandits bought a ranch near the Andes where they lived for several years. But a life of crime drew them back—it seemed easier than ranching. In 1908, they abandoned their ranch and headed north out of Argentina. After robbing a mining company in southern Bolivia, they were killed by Bolivian soldiers.

Languages

Spanish is the official language of Argentina. But at least seventeen languages are spoken regularly in the country. Apart from the indigenous languages, many Argentines also speak English, Italian, German, or French.

Argentine Spanish is different in some ways from the Spanish used in other Latin American countries. One of the most common changes is using *vos* instead of *tú*, to mean "you" when speaking to a close friend. Some Argentine words

Common Spanish Words and Phrases

Good morning	*Buenos días*
Hello	*Hola*
Please	*Por favor*
Thank you	*Gracias*
Good-bye	*Chau or Adios*
Do you speak English?	*¿Habla usted inglés?*

Hey, Che!

Ernesto "Che" Guevara, the Argentine revolutionary leader, got his nickname from being an Argentine. Argentines tend to call almost anyone—a friend, a taxi driver, a waiter—*che*, meaning something like "friend." It may derive from the Tehuelche word for "man."

started out as slang. For example, instead of the Spanish *chica* for "girl," they may say *china*. "Good" is *joya* instead of *bueno*. "Gasoline" is *nafta* instead of *gasolina*. Some people in Buenos Aires speak a special local slang called *lunfardo*. It is a blend of Spanish and Italian. Many of the words put the first syllable at the end, and the last syllable at the beginning. An example is *gotan* for *tango*.

The Gauchos

When the Spaniards first came to South America, few Spanish women came along. So, many of the first Spanish settlers had babies with indigenous women. Their descendants, called mestizos, usually have dark skin and hair. Many mestizos stayed in the frontier, where they were more accepted. The cities were populated mostly by people of European descent who looked down on the mestizos. Many mestizos worked with horses and cattle. They became the gauchos, or "cowboys," of Argentina.

The traditional gaucho was a great horseman. He wore baggy trousers tucked into his boots. He carried an elaborately carved knife called a *facón*. When pursuing horses or cattle, he used a *boleadora* (also called a *bola*). This consisted of three stones or metal balls wrapped in leather and connected by leather strips. The gaucho whirled the boleadora over his head

and then threw it at the legs of a running animal, bringing it down to the ground.

When they felt like it, gauchos worked on ranches. Otherwise, they would steal cattle and sell them. Some also kept their own wild herds in territories that became smaller as the ranches spread.

The gaucho became a romantic symbol in Argentina because of a long poem called *The Gaucho Martín Fierro*, which was written by José Hernández and published in 1872. It tells the story of a man who is simple, even lazy, but who has profound ideas on how people should get along.

Today, the traditional gauchos are gone. Now the gauchos are cowboys who work steadily on the ranches of the Pampas.

The word *gaucho* may come from the Quechua word for "orphan" or "wanderer."

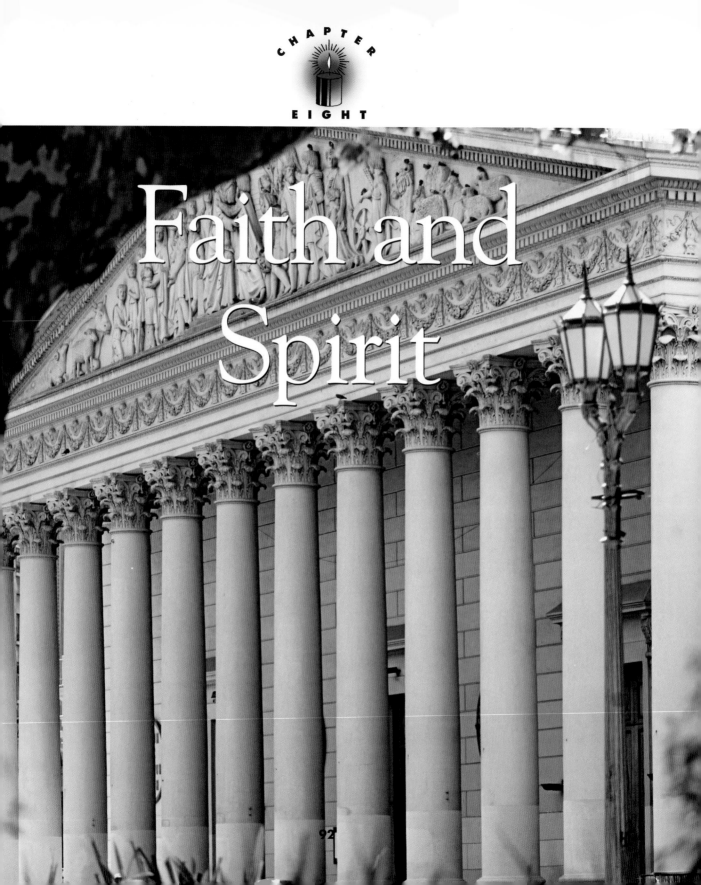

Faith and Spirit

Most Argentines are Roman Catholic. Until 1994, the president had to be Roman Catholic.

Opposite: **The Metropolitan Cathedral is the center of the Catholic Church in Buenos Aires.**

THE ROMAN CATHOLIC FAITH HAS DOMINATED Argentina since Catholic missionaries arrived in the early years of Spanish settlement. Argentina's national census, which counts the people in the country, does not ask about faith, so religious beliefs can only be estimated. More than 90 percent of Argentines say they are Roman Catholic, but less than one-fourth of them attend church regularly.

The Metropolitan Cathedral contains the tomb of José de San Martin. The "father of Argentina" died in France in 1850, but his remains were moved to Buenos Aires in 1880.

The Roman Catholic Church

Argentina's constitution says that Argentines are free to follow whatever religion they want. But the Roman Catholic Church gets special treatment in Argentina. The government pays the salaries of bishops and cardinals. It also supports many Catholic schools. In recent years, people have objected to this arrangement, and the church is considering giving up such financial support. Religion is a required subject in public schools, but parents are allowed to choose the faith being taught.

Carnaval!

Carnaval is a wild celebration held just before Lent, the period leading up to Easter when Christians are quiet and thoughtful. In Buenos Aires, parades filled with lively bands and colorful costumes take over the streets. The towns of Gualeguaychú and Corrientes are famed for their huge Carnaval celebrations.

Argentina's Religions

Religion	Percentage
Roman Catholic	92%
Protestant	2%
Jewish	2%
Other	4%

Religious festivals play a large role in many small towns and villages. During these festivals, Catholic statues are often carried through the streets.

In some cases, folk legend and religion have merged. One of the most popular stories concerns a woman named Deolinda Correa. According to legend, her husband was a soldier in the 1840 civil war. He became sick and she tried to reach him, but she died of starvation and thirst. Some soldiers found her body by the side of the road. Her baby was still nursing at her breast even though several days had passed. The soldiers called it a

The Virgin of Luján

Argentina's patron saint is the Virgin of Luján. According to legend, a wagon was carrying goods inland when it stopped dead. The oxen pulling the wagon refused to budge. The driver could not get them to move again until a small statue of Jesus's mother, the Virgin Mary, was taken out of the wagon. The statue was left behind where the town of Luján now stands. It is now housed in a large church, which is visited by millions of pilgrims every year.

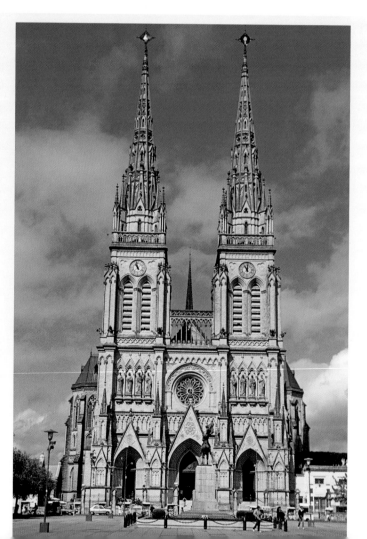

miracle and built a shrine where she was buried, at Vallecito in the western Pampas. Many Argentines make pilgrimages to her shrine to pray for miracles. The church disapproves of this, however.

The shrine of Deolinda Correa includes a life-size statue of the woman and her baby. An estimated two hundred thousand people visit the shrine each Easter.

Other Christian Groups

The first Protestants in Argentina were Scots who settled near Buenos Aires in 1815. For many years, the number of Protestants remained small. But since 1960, their numbers have been increasing more rapidly. The growing Protestant population is mostly among evangelical groups, which call for a strict interpretation of the Bible.

Argentina has about eighty synagogues, Jewish houses of worship.

Nearly three hundred thousand Mormons, members of the Church of Jesus Christ of Latter-day Saints, live in Argentina. They are the largest Christian group in Argentina apart from Roman Catholics.

Jews in Argentina

Many Jews immigrated to Argentina in the late nineteenth century. Today, Argentina has the largest Jewish population in Latin America. Most Jews live in Buenos Aires.

Discrimination against Jews, called anti-Semitism, is fairly common in Argentine society. Jews make up 2 percent of the Argentine population. But during the military junta of 1976 to 1983, about 10 percent of the people who were tortured or killed were Jews. After the junta's rule ended, historians discovered that many high-ranking Catholics had

Terrorism Against Jews

In 1992, a man drove a pickup truck packed with explosives into the front of the Israeli Embassy in Buenos Aires. The embassy, a neighboring Catholic church, and a school were destroyed. Twenty-nine people, only a few of them Israeli, were killed. Two years later, another bomb destroyed a building that served as the headquarters of Argentina's Jewish community. This time, eighty-five people were killed.

Every Monday since the second bombing, Jewish groups have gathered in front of the courts to demand that those responsible be found. No one has ever been arrested.

worked with the junta against Jews. Some of the Catholics apparently thought that the Jews were conspiring to set up a Jewish nation in Patagonia.

The King Fahd Islamic Cultural Center in Palermo contains the largest mosque in all of Latin America.

Muslim Communities

Muslims have been coming to Argentina since about 1850. Most arrived from Syria or Lebanon. Today, an estimated seven hundred thousand Argentines follow the religion of Islam. Carlos Saúl Menem, the son of Syrian immigrants, became Argentina's first Muslim president in 1989.

Opposite: **People in the village of Quebrado celebrate the Humahuaqueño carnival each year. The festival mixes Spanish traditions and the rituals of the Incas, the native people of Peru.**

Argentina's largest mosque—a Muslim house of worship—is in Palermo, a suburb of Buenos Aires. Its prayer hall can hold two thousand people.

Indigenous Religions

Indigenous people who have not been raised as Catholics often practice ancient religions. Traditionally, the Guaraní people recognized a supreme creator-god called Tupa. He made the Guaraní and then left them with lesser gods of good and evil. Though the Guaraní were early converts to Catholicism, even today many Guaraní villages have a prayer house and a traditional religious leader.

About a quarter of a million Mapuche people live in Argentina, mostly in the south. Their spiritual leader, who is usually a woman, is called the *machi*. The machi uses drums and other means to communicate with the spirits that create and sustain nature. Some machis are said to have healing powers.

Many people have moved to Argentina from neighboring countries in recent years. Some have brought their own traditional religions into the country.

Enjoying Sports and Arts

Young people kick a soccer ball around the Plaza del Congreso in downtown Buenos Aires.

ARGENTINES LOVE THEIR LEISURE TIME, AND THEY FILL it with the best of music, theater, art, and sports. The country's huge immigrant population has brought cultural influences from around the world.

The Playing Field

Sports are a vital part of Argentine life. Everywhere in Argentina, people watch sports on television, go to stadiums to root for their favorite teams, or head out to a field themselves. Soccer is the most popular sport by far. British sailors brought the game to Buenos Aires in about 1860. Today, soccer games are held in practically every park in every city, especially on weekend afternoons.

Opposite: **Passionate soccer fans paint their faces in Argentina's national colors.**

Their Greatest Player

Many people think Diego Maradona was the greatest soccer player of all time. Maradona was born in a slum near Buenos Aires in 1960. His talent was already earning him notice by age ten. In 1981, he joined the Boca Juniors, one of Argentina's top teams. He was so popular that when he agreed to move to Europe to play, the government tried to prevent him. He went anyway, playing in Spain and, later, Italy. Maradona led the Argentine team to victory in the 1986 World Cup. For many people, his wizardry with the ball during the tournament erased any doubt that he was the best player in the game. Later in his career, his reputation was damaged somewhat when he failed two drug tests. Maradona retired from soccer in 1997.

Every four years, soccer teams representing nations from around the world compete in the World Cup. Argentina won the World Cup in 1978 and 1986. The victory in 1978 was particularly sweet because that year the World Cup was held in Argentina. Fans went crazy.

Soccer games in Argentina can sometimes be dangerous. Organized groups of hooligans go to games carrying weapons, prepared to fight. A game with no violence in the audience is rare. Because of this, women and children seldom go to soccer games.

Women do, however, play soccer. In 2003, Argentina's team played in the Women's World Cup.

Argentina had great success at the 2004 Olympics. The men's soccer team won the gold medal—beating Paraguay 1–0 in the final—and was the first team to win the gold without giving up a single goal during the entire Olympic competition. Their basketball team also won the gold medal.

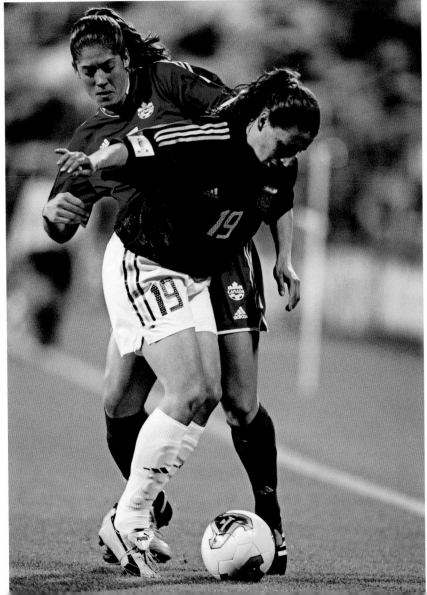

An Argentine player (in black) fights for the ball in a game against Canada during the 2003 Women's World Cup. Women's soccer is growing in popularity in Argentina.

The sport of polo shows off Argentina's great horses as well as their riders. In polo, teams of horseback riders hit a ball with long mallets, trying to get the ball into the opposing team's goal. Argentina is one of the few countries with professional polo teams.

Pato is a sport that is popular in Argentina but unknown in the United States. A combination of basketball and polo, pato involves players on horseback trying to get a ball through a basket. Pato got its start long ago with gauchos playing games with live ducks in baskets. The word *pato* is Spanish for "duck."

Pato players no long play with a duck. Instead, they try to get a leather ball with six handles into a hoop.

Out of the Ring

Luis Firpo was a boxer who popularized the sport of boxing in Argentina in the 1920s. Firpo, who was born in Junín in 1894, was called the "Wild Bull of the Pampas." He became the South American boxing champ in 1920. On September 14, 1923, he fought American heavyweight champ Jack Dempsey for the world champion title. Firpo hit Dempsey so hard that the American flew out of the ring and landed in the press box. That should have ended the fight, but Dempsey got back in the ring and knocked Firpo out. The referee, who had failed to end the fight, was suspended. Though Firpo never again had a world title fight, he was a hero in Latin America.

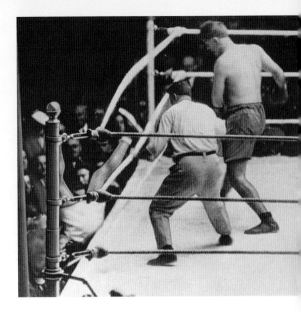

Playing Outdoors

Argentina has a long coastline, and many Argentines take full advantage of it. The beautiful beaches at Mar del Plata draw vacationers from all over Argentina. Other important coastal resorts are Necochea and Pinamar.

July and August are generally the best months to go skiing in Argentina. The snow is thick and powdery.

In southern Argentina, skiing is popular. Because seasons are opposite in the Southern Hemisphere, the prime ski season is June to October. Many skiers from North America head for the Patagonian resorts when it's warm back home.

A New Dance

In the 1880s, a type of music and dance called tango became popular in Buenos Aires. At first, only the lower classes did this dance because it involved the man's and woman's bodies touching each other. This was something that was simply not done in polite society. The tango was not accepted by the Argentine middle and upper classes until it became popular in Europe and then returned home. The tango, with its great drama and elegance, is again popular today.

The Musical Beat

Instruments from all over the world play a part in Argentine music. Indigenous people from the Andes developed a bass drum called the *bombo legüero*. It is often used as the basic instrument in Argentine folk music. The body of the drum is a hollowed-out log. The fur is left on the animal hide used for the drumhead. This gives the bombo legüero a darker and mellower sound than most drums.

The *bandoneón* is an accordion-like instrument invented in Germany. Also called the concertina, it quickly became more famous in Argentina for its use with the tango and other dances.

Carlos Gardel was the world's most famous tango singer. Born in France, he was taken to Argentina as a toddler. He began as a folksinger but soon switched to tango, which he helped popularize. During the 1930s, he moved to New York, where he sang on radio and in the movies. He died in a plane crash in 1935, but his music remains immensely popular throughout Latin America.

Tango composer Astor Piazzolla modernized the tango by including some elements of jazz. Various composers of classical music have included tango rhythms in symphonies and ballets.

Most bandoneóns have 71 buttons, which can produce a total of 142 notes. Each button plays a different note depending on whether the instrument is being pushed or pulled.

Classical music is important in Argentina. Both the National Symphony Orchestra and the National Ballet perform at the Colón Opera House. The beautiful seven-story building took eighteen years to build because all the materials were imported from Europe. It finally opened in 1908. Its gold and red interior seats 2,437, and an additional 4,000 people can stand.

The Colón Opera House is famed for its perfect sound.

The Great Conductor

Daniel Barenboim, a classical pianist and symphony conductor, was born in Buenos Aires in 1942 to Russian-Jewish parents. His family moved to Israel when he was ten years old, and he became a citizen of Israel. In the 1960s, he was scheduled to perform in Buenos Aires. The government refused to allow him into the country, however, because he had never served in the Argentine military, and service was mandatory at that time. He was allowed back in the 1990s after the laws were changed. He even recorded a CD of tango music. In 1991, Barenboim became the conductor of the Chicago Symphony Orchestra, a position he held until 2006.

One of Argentina's most famous classical composers, Alberto Williams, has been called the "father of Argentine national music." Many of his pieces reflect the danceable rhythms of the country. Another composer, Alberto Ginastera, wrote piano solos, sometimes incorporating Argentine rhythms. He wrote many orchestral works, including scores for eleven movies.

José Cura is a world-famous tenor who sings opera and is a conductor. Born in Rosario in 1962, he has worked with operas and orchestras worldwide. He has been singing with New York's Metropolitan Opera since 1999.

Rock and roll is popular
in Argentina.

Popular Music

Rock music is popular in Argentina. Among the top per-
formers is Charly Garcia, who is known for his gravelly
voice. As elsewhere, popular bands and music styles come
and go. In the 1980s, a band called Sumo performed rock
and reggae in English. The band came to an end when
its founder, Italian-born Luca Prodan, died in 1987. The
1990s brought *cumbia*, a type of music that began among
the poor classes and gained popularity among urban teen-
agers. *Cuarteto* is a type of upbeat dance music that began
in the 1940s with four-piece dance-hall bands. Rodrigo was
a famous cuarteto band in the 1990s.

Many Argentines also enjoy folk music, which often mixes with rock. Mercedes Sosa, who grew up in Tucumán, is famed for her powerful voice. Increasingly popular is Soledad Pastorutti, who was born in 1980 in Casilda. She gave her first public concerts at age fifteen and draws huge crowds wherever she performs.

The Written Word

It seems that Argentines are always reading. They read newspapers, magazines, and novels. But Argentina's writers have often faced difficulties. Many have had to flee the country because their writing offended the nation's military leaders.

José Mármol, born in 1818, is regarded as Argentina's first novelist. He wrote against dictator Juan Manuel de Rosas, who had him imprisoned briefly. Mármol's novel *La Amalia*, published in several parts between 1851 and 1855, had his characters living under Rosas's tyranny.

Julio Cortázar, novelist, poet, and short-story writer, was born in 1914. Much of his writing bordered on the fantastic because it followed the strange paths the human mind can take. He actively protested against dictator Juan Perón and eventually left Argentina for France, where he lived out his life.

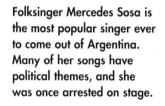

Folksinger Mercedes Sosa is the most popular singer ever to come out of Argentina. Many of her songs have political themes, and she was once arrested on stage.

Enjoying Sports and Arts **113**

The work of Jorge Luis Borges is filled with playful language and philosophical ideas.

In 1976, Manuel Puig (1932–1990) wrote *Kiss of the Spider Woman*, about two men sharing a prison cell during the dictatorship. It became a movie in 1985 and a Broadway musical in 1993.

Jorge Luis Borges, who was born in Buenos Aires in 1899, has been called the most important figure in all of Latin American literature. Many people feel that Borges should have received the Nobel Prize for Literature, the world's highest literary honor. Though also a poet, he was best known for his short stories, collected in books such as *Everything and Nothing* and *Labyrinths*. *The Book of Imaginary Beings* is a collection of brief essays on the fabulous creatures of myth and legend. Borges died in 1986.

Mysteries have long been popular in Argentina. Some of Argentina's most respected literary writers also wrote mysteries for the fun of it. Borges and Adolf Bioy Casares developed a crime series together called the Seventh Circle. Writing together, they called themselves H. Bustos Domecq.

One of today's most acclaimed writers of mysteries and other stories is Luisa Valenzuela. Some of her short stories were published before she was twenty years old. Valenzuela first became famous in France and the United States, where she lived in exile during the junta years.

A Leader of Women

Writer Victoria Ocampo (1890–1979) was born in Buenos Aires and raised in France. Through her writing and speeches, she was influential in obtaining rights and recognition for women. Although she was glad that Juan Perón promised women the right to vote, she openly opposed him. She spoke out against his rule in *Sur* (*South*), the literary magazine she had founded in 1931. She was arrested in 1953 and jailed until public protests won her release. Ocampo was the first woman named to the Argentine Academy of Letters.

Argentina has long had a strong filmmaking industry. One of the country's most famous filmmakers is Leopoldo Torre Nilsson, who made movies from the 1940s to the 1970s. Argentine movies are rarely seen outside the country. In 1985, Director Luis Puenzo's film *The Official Story* received an Academy Award in Hollywood for best foreign film. The story concerns a family whose adopted daughter may have been the child of one of the disappeareds.

In recent years, the number of neighborhood movie theaters has shrunk. Many of the ones that remain show Hollywood movies because they need to draw large crowds.

People stream out of a theater showing *Kiss of the Spider Woman (El Beso del La Mujer Araña)*. The acclaimed movie was directed by Hector Babenco, who grew up in Buenos Aires.

"Don't Cry for Me, Argentina"

The 1978 musical *Evita*, based on the life of Eva Duarte de Perón, was made into a film starring Madonna in 1996. President Carlos Saúl Menem did not decide until the cast and crew got to Buenos Aires whether the Casa Rosada could be used for filming. Madonna went to Menem directly and asked if they could film where the real Evita had spoken to Perón's followers. He agreed. Standing on the balcony, Madonna sang the most popular song from the musical, "Don't Cry for Me, Argentina."

Argentine TV productions are shown throughout Latin America and on some Hispanic cable stations in the United States. Sports programs are hugely popular, as are soap operas.

Like Americans, Argentines like reality shows. One of the most popular is *Camera in Hand*, in which interviewers follow celebrities to important events and record the whole thing by hidden camera. Viewers also enjoy variety shows. Susana Giménez is the host of a successful show, called simply *Susana Giménez*. It has been running for nineteen years.

Actor Segundo Cernadas, a native of Río Negro, is a teen idol on television programs, especially soap operas. His show *Kiss Me, Fool* began to appear on the U.S. Univision channel in 2004.

Life Throughout the Year

LAS 24 HS.

Argentina has a good school system. More than 97 percent of adults can read and write.

I N ARGENTINA, CHILDREN GO TO SCHOOL IN FALL, WINTER, and spring, just as they do in North America. But in Argentina, those seasons run from February to November. Christmas falls during summer vacation. Santa Claus must swelter in the heat!

Education

Domingo Faustino Sarmiento, who was president of Argentina from 1862 to 1869, said that all Argentines must go to school. The day of Sarmiento's death, September 11, is celebrated as Teacher's Day. Today, young Argentines are required to go to school through the ninth grade. School is free up to that point. High school lasts several years.

Opposite: A quarter of the people in Argentina are less than fifteen years old.

On Graduating

On graduating from high school, those students who can afford it take a trip called the *viaje de egresados*, meaning "school-leaving trip." The celebrating students fly to Bariloche on Lake Nahuel Huapi where they dance and ski for days, or they may go climbing together in the mountains. In 2004, the Argentine Ministry of Education began to fund these trips for low-income students.

Students attend class at a rural school near Córdoba.

Many ranches in the Pampas—where the nearest town is far away—hold classes for the children of the ranch owners and workers. Argentine schoolchildren wear white cotton jackets over their regular clothing when they are in class.

Public support of education has fallen in recent years. More than half of Argentines quit school as soon as they are legally allowed, after ninth grade.

Argentina has more than seventy-five universities. The oldest is the University of Córdoba, which was founded in 1613. The largest college in the nation, the University of Buenos Aires, has more than 175,000 students. About half of the universities are publicly owned and are free to students.

College students tend to go to colleges near their homes and live at home while in school. More than half the university students are women, and more women than men are now graduating from medical school and becoming doctors. Women are less likely than men to move to the top in business or politics, however.

City Life, Country Life

The lives of the *porteños*, the people of Buenos Aires, are very different from the lives of the people who live in the interior. The two groups rarely mix.

Buenos Aires has one of the largest middle classes in Latin America. Many people there work in offices, eat in restaurants, and go shopping. Porteños take great pride in their looks and how they dress. Unfortunately, this has helped to contribute

The Quinceañera

Many Argentine girls celebrate their fifteenth birthday with an event called the *quinceañera*. The birthday girl wears white at her big party, which marks the end of childhood and the start of adulthood.

to a high incidence of anorexia and bulimia in Argentina. People with anorexia starve themselves or overexercise in order to be thin.

Some porteños have enough money that they can afford their own country house, usually within an hour outside of Buenos Aires. Called *quintas*, these homes are often grouped together around country clubs. Even out in the country, the porteños rarely socialize with the people of the interior.

But not everyone in Buenos Aires lives so well. Large shantytowns, or slums, surround the city. Most slum dwellers came to Buenos Aires from the Interior or immigrated from

Some modern country houses offer a pleasant retreat from bustling Buenos Aires.

neighboring countries. They build the shacks they live in with whatever material they can find—old wood, tin, or even mud. If they are lucky, there is a pipe of fresh water running through the community.

About 12 percent of Argentines live in rural areas. They are generally poorer than people in the cities. Wealthy landowners live in large, fancy houses. But most people live in small houses with mud-brick walls and dirt floors.

In the interior, away from Buenos Aires, people still enjoy the siesta, an afternoon rest. Businesses close for several hours in the afternoon so that people can sleep through the worst heat of the day. The siesta allows them to stay up late at night and still work the next day. Some shops, restaurants, and dance halls are open all night.

Slums circle Buenos Aires. An estimated one-third of Argentines live in poverty.

Many Argentine restaurants add a decoration or pattern on empanadas to show what kind of filling they have. These empanadas are filled with fish.

Argentina is famous for its cattle, and Argentines love their beef. It is estimated that Argentines eat about three times as much red meat as Americans. Family get-togethers on Sunday afternoons always feature *asado*, beef grilled on an outdoor barbeque. A popular meat dish for picnics is *empanadas*, bread filled with good beef. Empanadas can also be filled with vegetables, cheese, or fruit. A favorite sweet is the *alfajor*, two cookies with chocolate or caramel in between. It is dipped in melted chocolate before eating.

An Argentine Asado

Asado—beef cooked on an outdoor grill—should be accompanied by a sauce called *chimichurri*. Mix the following ingredients together earlier in the day or even the day before, and put the mixture in the refrigerator. When you are ready to cook, brush this chimichurri on the meat. Add more after the meat is grilled.

$\frac{1}{2}$ cup virgin olive oil

$\frac{1}{2}$ cup white wine vinegar

1 onion, diced

4 garlic cloves, pressed

$\frac{1}{2}$ cup fresh parsley, chopped

1 teaspoon thyme

1 tablespoon lemon juice

Salt and cayenne pepper to taste

A Friendly Mate

Mate (pronounced MAH-tay) is a drink made from the dried leaves of the yerba mate plant. (*Yerba* means "herb," and *mate* means "cup," so *yerba mate* means "herb cup.") People say yerba mate gives the body energy and makes the mind alert. Argentines drink yerba mate through a *bombilla*, a metal straw with a spoon-shaped filter at the end. Most Argentines drink mate. People in the north tend to sweeten the drink, while those elsewhere like it unsweetened. It's said that Argentines use 200,000 tons of yerba mate each year.

Italian restaurants are popular in Argentina. Many Italians immigrated to Argentina, bringing their food tastes along with them.

Reasons to Celebrate

Throughout the year, Argentines find many reasons to celebrate. May 25, Revolution Day, is celebrated like the Fourth of July in the United States. The day features parades and fireworks, which commemorate Argentina becoming self-governing in 1810. Argentine Independence Day, July 9, celebrates its actual independence from Spain, achieved in 1816.

National Holidays

January 1	New Year's Day
March or April	Good Friday
March or April	Easter
April 2	Day of Veterans and Fallen in Malvinas (Falklands) War
May 1	Labor Day
May 25	Revolution Day (Anniversary of the First National Government)
June 20	Day of the National Flag
July 9	Independence Day
August 17	Anniversary of the Death of General José de San Martín
September 11	Teacher's Day
October 12	Day of the Americas; also called Race Day
December 8	Day of the Immaculate Conception
December 25	Christmas

Famous people who have died are honored on the day of their death rather than the day on which they were born. For example, San Martín is remembered on the anniversary of his death, August 17, not on his birthday. A special gaucho day, called Tradition Day, is held in November at San Antonio de Areco. Tango is a big part of the National Folklore Festival at Cosquín in January.

The Need to Talk

Argentines tend to be a talkative, joyful people who celebrate life by talking about it. Conversations are held—loudly— on street corners, in restaurants, and wherever people pass. Small cafés, called *confiterías*, abound. Almost every city block has at least one. A great deal of social and business life happens at one's local café. Politics and sports are favorite topics of conversation. Discussions can go on all night long because, like many Spanish countries, Argentina's cities offer nightlife that doesn't stop.

Perhaps because Argentines enjoy talking so much, many of them visit psychologists to talk about themselves. Argentina has the second-highest number of psychologists per person of any country in the world. Many Argentine psychologists also practice in other Spanish-speaking countries.

An ever-important topic of discussion, whether in a café or with a psychologist, is what it means to be Argentine. Are Argentines Europeans? Latin Americans? How are they different from other people? Is that difference important? Why have they had so many periods of dictatorship in their history? What does their willingness to accept dictatorships say about them? Is that willingness now a thing of the past? Argentines never stop talking about these questions—unfortunately, many of these questions have no answers.

Argentines are great talkers.

Timeline

Argentine History

Early people create farming settlements in **ca. 5000** B.C. what is now Argentina.

Explorer Juan Díaz de Solís claims A.D. **1516**
Argentina for Spain.

Ferdinand Magellan explores the Río de **1520**
la Plata and sails around Patagonia and
Tierra del Fuego.

Argentina's first permanent town, Santiago **1553**
del Estero, is founded.

Buenos Aires is founded for the second time. **1580**

Spain creates the Viceroyalty of Río de la **1776**
Plata, with Buenos Aires as the capital.

Argentina forms a government **1810**
independent of Spain but still declares
itself loyal to the Spanish king.

World History

2500 B.C.	Egyptians build the pyramids and the Sphinx in Giza.
563 B.C.	The Buddha is born in India.
A.D. 313	The Roman emperor Constantine legalizes Christianity.
610	The Prophet Muhammad begins preaching a new religion called Islam.
1054	The Eastern (Orthodox) and Western (Roman Catholic) Churches break apart.
1095	The Crusades begin.
1215	King John seals the Magna Carta.
1300s	The Renaissance begins in Italy.
1347	The plague sweeps through Europe.
1453	Ottoman Turks capture Constantinople, conquering the Byzantine Empire.
1492	Columbus arrives in North America.
1500s	Reformers break away from the Catholic Church, and Protestantism is born.
1776	The Declaration of Independence is signed.
1789	The French Revolution begins.

Argentine History

Argentina becomes totally independent of Spain.	1816
Civil War breaks out between people favoring and opposing a strong central government.	1819
Great Britain occupies the Falkland Islands.	1833
Argentina's constitution is approved; slavery is abolished.	1853
Buenos Aires becomes Argentina's capital.	1862
Argentina, Brazil, and Uruguay fight Paraguay in the War of the Triple Alliance.	1864–1870
Settlers move to western and southern Argentina in the Conquest of the Desert.	1860–1885
Millions of immigrants arrive from Europe.	1885–1920
Argentina suffers during the worldwide depression, and the military takes control.	1930
Juan Perón begins his rise to power.	1944
Eva Perón dies of cancer.	1952
The military overthrows Juan Perón, who flees the country.	1955
Perón returns to Argentina as president.	1973
Perón dies; his third wife, Isabel Martinez de Perón, becomes president, but chaos follows.	1974
The Dirty War begins.	1976
Argentine troops invade the Falkland Islands; British troops force them out.	1982
Civilian rule returns to Argentina.	1983
Argentina's economy collapses.	2001
Argentina defaults on international loans; the peso is devalued, leaving millions in poverty.	2002
The Supreme Court agrees to allow leaders of the Dirty War to be put on trial.	2005

World History

1865	The American Civil War ends.
1879	The first practical light bulb is invented.
1914	World War I breaks out.
1917	The Bolshevik Revolution brings communism to Russia.
1929	A worldwide economic depression begins.
1939	World War II begins.
1945	World War II ends.
1957	The Vietnam War starts.
1969	Humans land on the Moon.
1975	The Vietnam War ends.
1989	The Berlin Wall is torn down as communism crumbles in Eastern Europe.
1991	The Soviet Union breaks into separate states.
2001	Terrorists attack the World Trade Center, New York, and the Pentagon, Washington, D.C.

Fast Facts

Official name: *República Argentine* (Argentine Republic)

Capital: Buenos Aires

Official language: Spanish

Córdoba

Argentina's flag

Jaguar

Official religion:	None, but the Roman Catholic Church has a special relationship with the state	
National anthem:	"¡Oid, Mortales!" ("Hear, O Mortals!")	
Type of government:	Federal republic	
Head of government:	President	
Area:	1,068,020 square miles (2,765,958 sq km)	
Geographic center:	34°00' South, 64°00' West	
Bordering countries:	Chile, Bolivia, Paraguay, Brazil, Uruguay	
Highest elevation:	Mount Aconcagua, 22,835 feet (6,960 m)	
Lowest elevation:	Laguna del Carbón, 345 feet (105 m) below sea level	

Average high temperatures:

	in January	in July
Northeastern Argentina	95°F (35°C)	73°F (23°C)
Buenos Aires	84°F (29°C)	57°F (14°C)
Southern Argentina	70°F (21°C)	43°F (6°C)

Annual rainfall range:	8–80 inches (20–200 cm)
National population (2005 est.):	39,537,943
System of weights and measures:	Metric

Plaza de Mayo

Population of largest cities (2005 est.):

Buenos Aires	11,600,000
Córdoba	1,450,000
Rosario	1,200,000
Mendoza	1,003,000
La Plata	810,000

Famous landmarks:

- ▶ *Iguazú Falls*, Misiones province
- ▶ *La Plata Cathedral*, La Plata
- ▶ *Perito Moreno Glacier*, Patagonia
- ▶ *Cave of the Hands*, Patagonia
- ▶ *Casa Rosada*, Buenos Aires
- ▶ *Plaza de Mayo*, Buenos Aires

Industry: Manufacturing plays a large part in the Argentine economy. Automobiles, textiles, and food products are among the leading products. Oil is the country's leading mineral resource, and oil refining is also an important industry. Beef, corn, and wheat are among the country's top farm products. Though Argentina's economy is well developed and diverse, in recent years it has sometimes been unstable, causing extreme inflation.

Currency: The Argentine peso, which is divided into 100 centavos. In 2006, three pesos equaled one U.S. dollar.

Literacy: 97.5%

Currency

Rural schoolchildren

Ernesto "Che" Guevara

Common words and phrases:		
	Buenos días	Good morning
	Hola	Hello
	Por favor	Please
	Gracias	Thank you
	Chau or *Adios*	Good-bye
	¿Habla usted inglés?	Do you speak English?

Famous Argentines:		
	Daniel Barenboim	(1942–)
	Pianist and conductor	
	Jorge Luis Borges	(1899–1986)
	Writer	
	Carlos Gardel	(1890–1935)
	Tango singer	
	Alberto Ginastera	(1916–1983)
	Classical music composer	
	Ernesto "Che" Guevara	(1928–1967)
	Revolutionary hero	
	Néstor Kirchner	(1950–)
	President	
	Diego Maradona	(1960–)
	Soccer player	
	Victoria Ocampo	(1890–1979)
	Feminist leader and writer	
	Eva Duarte de Perón	(1919–1952)
	First lady	
	Juan Domingo Perón	(1895–1974)
	President and dictator	
	José de San Martín	(1778–1850)
	Military hero	

To Find Out More

Nonfiction

▶ Crooker, Richard A. *Argentina*. Philadelphia: Chelsea House, 2003.

▶ Dingus, Lowell, and Luis Chiappe. *The Tiniest Giants: Discovering Dinosaur Eggs*. New York: Doubleday, 1999.

▶ Dougherty, Terri. *Argentina*. San Diego: Lucent, 2003.

▶ Fearns, Les, and Daisy Fearns. *Argentina*. New York: Facts on File, 2005.

▶ Furstinger, Nancy. *Buenos Aires*. Edina, MN: Checkerboard Books, 2005.

▶ Link, Theodore, and Rose McCarthy. *Argentina: A Primary Source Cultural Guide*. New York: PowerPlus Books, 2004.

▶ Lourie, Peter. *Tierra del Fuego: A Journey to the End of the Earth*. Honesdale, PA: Boyds Mills Press, 2002.

▶ Stille, Darlene R. *Eva Perón: First Lady of Argentina*. Minneapolis: Compass Point Books, 2006.

Fiction

▶ Kalnay, Francis. *Chúcaro: Wild Pony of the Pampa*. New York: Walker, 1993.

▶ Slaughter, Charles H. *The Dirty War: A Novel*. New York: Walker, 1994.

▶ Thornton, Lawrence. *Imagining Argentina*. New York: Doubleday, 1987.

DVDs

▶ *Discovering Argentina: Dinosaurs*. Discoveries series. Bennett-Watt Media, 2001.

▶ *Discovering Argentina: Nature's Spectacle*. Discoveries series. Bennett-Watt Media, 2002.

▶ *Globe Trekker: Argentina*. 555 Productions, 2004.

▶ *Imagining Argentina*. MCA Home Video, 2005.

Web Sites

▶ **Argentina's Ministry of Tourism**
www.turismo.gov.ar/eng/menu.htm
For all sorts of information from the Argentine government.

▶ **Argentina Turistica**
www.argentinaturistica.com
For travel information and basic facts.

▶ **BBC News: Argentina Profile**
http://news.bbc.co.uk/1/hi/world/
americas/country_profiles/1192478.stm
For an overview of facts and current news.

▶ **Buenos Aires Herald**
www.buenosairesherald.com
To read the country's largest and oldest international newspaper.

Organizations and Embassies

▶ **Consulate General and Promotion Center of Argentina in New York**
12 West 56th Street
New York, NY 10019
212-603-0400

▶ **Embassy of the Argentine Republic**
1600 New Hampshire Avenue, NW
Washington, DC 20009
202-238-6400

Index

Page numbers in *italics* indicate illustrations.

oil, 74
Old Patagonian Express, 78, *78*
*Old Patagonian Express: By Train
    through the Americas, The* (Paul
    Theroux), 78
Olympic Games, 105
ombú trees, 41, *41*
Onganía, Juan Carlos, 55
ovenbird (national bird), 38, 66

P

Palermo, 100
Pampas region, 9, *9*, 10, 11, 16,
    22–23, 24, 29, 34, 39, 41, 47, 48,
    50, 51, 120
Pampas cat, 32
pamperos winds, 28
Paraná River, 17, 18, 22, 23
Parera, José Blas, 67
Parker, Robert Leroy, 89, *89*
Pastorutti, Soledad, 113
Patagonia region, 10–11, *10*, 14, 16,
    18, 25–26, *25*, 29, 37, 39, 40, 43,
    51, 86, 87, 89
Patagonian cavies. *See* maras.
Patagonian hares, 35
pato (sport), 106, *106*
peccaries, 32, 36, *36*
people
    campesinos, 11
    children, 56, 84, 104, *118*, 119,
        119, 120, *120*, 121
    clothing, 90, 120, 122
    conversation, 126–127, *127*
    Disappeareds, 56, *56*, 57–58, 59,
        116
    education, 94, 119–121, *119*, *120*
    estancieros (land-owning elite), 72
    Europeans, 12
    food, 72, 86, 88, *88*, 124–125
    gauchos, 39–40, 49, 90–91, *91*
    Guaraní, 43–44, 51, 86, 100

Hispanics, 11
homelessness, *81*
housing, 70, 122, *122*, 123, *123*
immigrants, 52, *52*, 69, 84, 85,
    87–88
indigenous, 20, 23, 39–40, 43–44,
    45, 47, 49, 51, 62, 83, 84–85,
    85, 86–87, 90, 100, 108
Mapuche, 27, 86, 100
Mbya community, 85–86
mestizos, 83, 87, 90
middle class, 65, 122
Montoneros, 55
nomads, 44
population, 83
porteños, 11, 68, 121–122
Quilmes, 42
quinceañera (fifteenth birthday), 121
"shirtless, the," 54
siestas, 123
Tehuelche, 25
vacations, *16*, 107
women, 54, 56, 64, 90, 100, 104,
    105, *105*, 114, 121, 122
Perón, Eva Duarte de, 53, 54, *54*, 117
Perón, Isabel Martínez de, 55
Perón, Juan Domingo, 53–55, *53*, 65,
    113, 114
Piazzolla, Astor, 109
Pinamar, 107
plant life, *10*, 21, 22, 23, 41
Plaza de Mayo, 56, 68
Plaza del Congreso, *102*
Plaza Dorrego, 69
polo, 106
population, 83
population density map, 84
porteño people, 11, 68, 121–122
poverty, 58, 80, 81, *81*, 123, *123*
Prodan, Luca, 112
Protestantism, 96, 97
provinces, 61, 63

pudus, 35, *35*
Puenzo, Luis, 116
Puig, Manuel, 114
pumas, 31–32, *31*, 34

Q

quebracho trees, 21
Quebrado, *101*
Quechua language, 22, 86
Quilmes people, *42*
quinceañera (fifteenth birthday), 121
quintas (houses), 122, *122*

R

Radical Civic Union, 65
railroads, 78
rain forests, 40
ranching, 52, 72
recipe, 124
religion
    holidays, 95
    Humahuaqueño carnival, *101*
    indigenous people, 100
    Islamic, 99–100
    Judaism, 96, 98–99
    machi (spiritual leader), 100
    Metropolitan Cathedral, *92*, 94
    Mormons, 98
    mosques, 99, 100
    Protestantism, 96, 97
    Roman Catholicism, 46–47, 62,
        92, 93, *93*, 94, 96, 98, 99
    synagogues, 98
reptilian life, 37
Revolution Day, 125
rheas, 39
rhodochrosite, 66
Río de la Plata, 11–12, 17, *17*, 24,
    8, 44, 45, 68
Roca, Julio A., 51
rock music, 112, *112*
rodents, 32, *32*, 34–35, *34*, *35*, 37

Meet the Author

J EAN F. BLASHFIELD has been fascinated by Argentina her entire life. Even as a child she was intrigued by the thought that Santa Claus came in summer, and that while she was enjoying a vacation at the beach, Argentines were skiing. And she was certain that Patagonia must be one of the truly wonderful places of the earth.

Jean F. Blashfield delights in learning lots of fascinating, though not always important, things about places and the people who live in them. When writing a book for young people, she's often as challenged by what to leave out as what to put in.

She has been a traveler since she first went on a college choir tour of Europe. She was determined she would again go overseas. After developing the *Young People's Science Encyclopedia* for Children's Press, she kept that promise to herself and moved to London. That city became her headquarters for three years of travel throughout Europe. It was in London that she first began to write books for young people.

Since then, she has written more than 130 books. She likes best to write about interesting places, but she loves history, science, and almost every other topic. She has created an encyclopedia of aviation and space, written popular books on murderers and house plants, and had a lot of fun creating a book on women's exploits called *Hellraisers, Heroines, and Holy Women*. She was the founder of the Dungeons & Dragons book department at TSR, Inc., and became avidly interested in medieval history.

Jean Blashfield was born in Madison, Wisconsin. She graduated from the University of Michigan and worked for publishers in Chicago and Washington, D.C. She returned to the Lake Geneva area in southern Wisconsin when she married Wallace Black (a publisher, writer, and pilot) and began to raise a family. She has two children in graduate school, two cats, and two computers in her home in Delavan. In addition to researching via her computers, she produces whole books on the computer—scanning pictures, creating layouts, and even developing the index. She has become an avid Internet surfer and is working on her own Web site, but she'll never give up her trips to the library, or to other countries.

Photo Credits